CW01669742

THE SECRET LORE OF PLANTS AND FLOWERS

By The Same Author

The Dark World of Witches
The Realm of Ghosts
The Domain of Devils
Magic Medicine and Quackery
Superstition and the Superstitious
Witchcraft: The Story of Man's Quest for Supernatural Power
Deadly Magic
Supernatural England

Paths to Inner Power Series:
The Magic of Perfume
Incantations and Words of Power
The Ancient Art of Occult Healing

With Lynn Myring
Haunted Houses

With Eliot Humberstone
Mysterious Powers

THE SECRET LORE OF PLANTS AND FLOWERS

Eric Maple

With illustrations by
Valerie Croker

ROBERT HALE LIMITED
LONDON

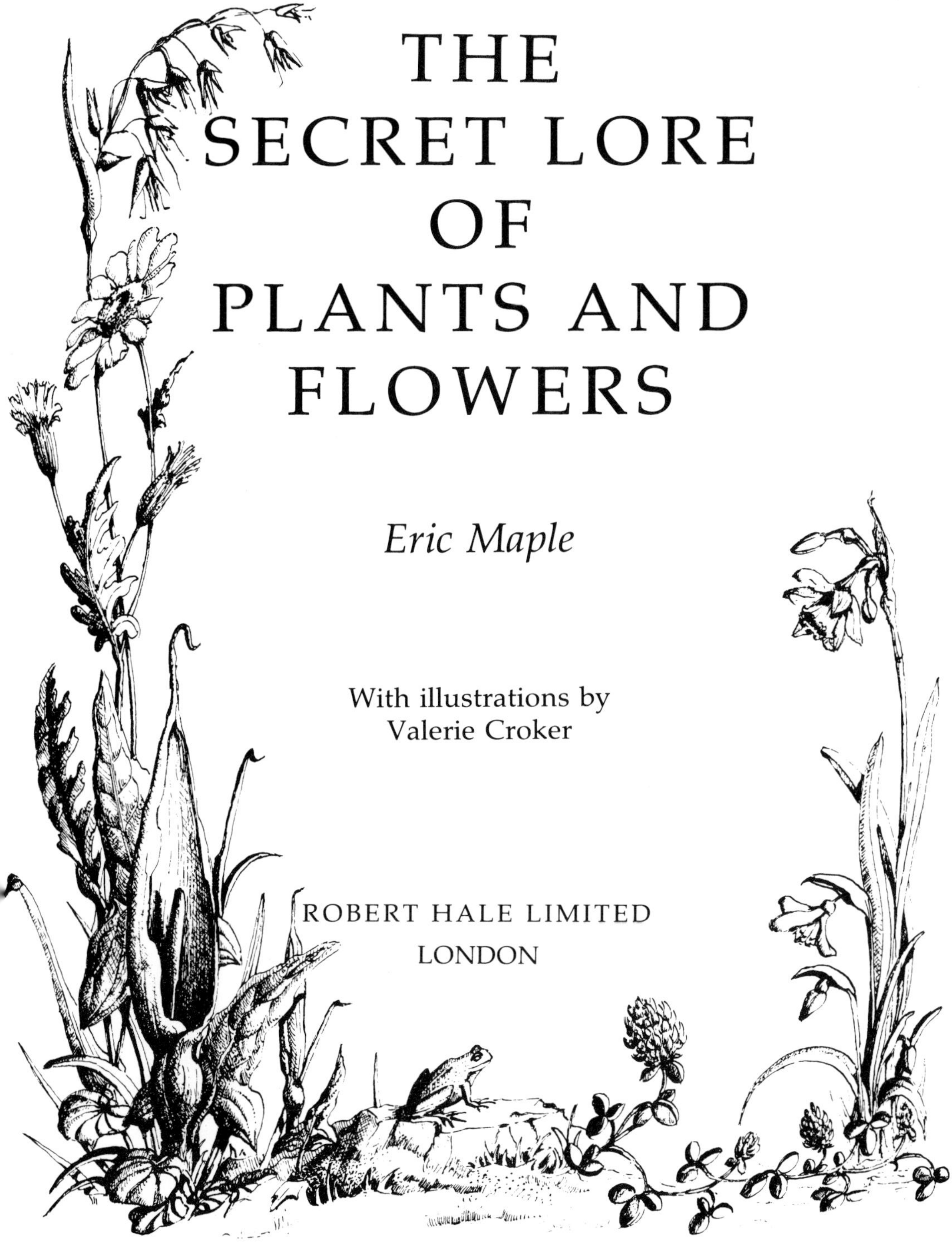

The author acknowledges, with thanks, the following who have given permission for reproduction of quotations from books in copyright: Weidenfeld & Nicolson, *Aphrodisiacs in Your Garden* by Charles Connell; Frederick Warne Publishers Ltd, *A Flower-Lover's Miscellany* by Daphne Barraclough; Cassell Ltd, *Gardens of Delight* by Miles and John Hadfield; Curtis Brown Ltd, *Fringe Medicine* by Brian Inglis; The Aquarian Press and Charles Bowness, *Romany Magic* by Charles Bowness.

Copyright © Eric Maple 1980
First published in Great Britain 1980

ISBN 0 7091 8125 6

Robert Hale Limited,
Clerkenwell House,
Clerkenwell Green,
LONDON EC1R 0HT

Photoset, printed and bound
in Great Britain by
REDWOOD BURN LIMITED
Trowbridge & Esher

Contents

Illustrations

Pan's Garden

Preface

I remember once reading about a day-dreamer and nature lover who sat in an English meadow on a warm summer's afternoon where, believing himself unheard, he suddenly declared, "If only the wild flowers could be changed just for one single day into people – what a fascinating spectacle we should see."

This remarkable soliloquy is not so out of this world as it might at first appear, although very few flower lovers are aware that at an early period in the human story happenings of this kind were accepted everywhere as a matter of course. In those days maidens were transformed into flowers at the whim of a god, or at the touch of a witch's wand, while country folk searched the woodlands and hedgerows for magical panaceas thoughtfully provided by nature for their ills and chills. There existed – if the old legends are to be taken as true – many divine flowers which were worshipped, as well as sinister ones which were shunned by everyone other than witches, warlocks and the ill-disposed.

Folklore, the traditional lore of the people, offers a treasure trove of fascinating information relating to the legends of plants, trees and flowers inherited from earlier generations. Charlotte Burne discusses the subject at length in her invaluable book, *A Handbook Of Folklore,* in a somewhat prosaically-titled chapter "The Vegetable World" from which comes the following quotation: "Man from the earliest times must have been indebted to trees and plants for food, shelter, fuel and clothing. In the search for edible plants and fruits he could not fail to become acquainted also with the poisonous narcotic or medicinal qualities of other plants. Between need, fear and the sense of mystery, the growth of myth and ritual would be practically inevitable."

The world in which we live is so overwhelmed by materialism that we are in grave danger of losing that sense of wonder and mystery which adds an extra dimension to life. In this brief study of some of the earlier beliefs relating to trees, flowers and plants both domestic and wild, I hope to restore a little of our lost faith in the magic of the everyday world.

CHAPTER ONE

Flower Lore – A Secret History

> Little flower – but *if* I could understand
> What you are, root and all, and all in all,
> I should know what God and man is.
>
> "Flower in the Crannied Wall"
> *Tennyson*

To love flowers is to love all creation yet, strange to say, any appreciation of the qualities of the floral world seems to have been a comparatively late development in the history of mankind. From evidence which has survived it appears that our earlier ancestors took a distinctly pragmatic attitude towards the plants of the fields and woodlands, valuing them strictly in accordance with their supposed usefulness to society whether in the form of food, medicine or magic. Nevertheless, even from the earliest times flowers seem to have been credited with personalities of a semi-human character, such is the inherent tendency of men and women to endow nature with concepts and feelings somewhat like their own.

The human being's relationship with the environment was shaped by necessity; it was a continuous struggle to survive in a threatening world. Consequently, plants, trees and flowers were regarded as either friends, enemies or neutrals, and this explains the curious names by which they were known in the various localities. That invaluable source book, Geoffrey Grigson's *The*

Englishman's Flora, which lists the plants under their local names as distinct from their scientific and English ones, contains such gems of appreciation of nature's bounty as God Almighty's bread and cheese (wood-sorrel) and God's fingers and thumbs (lady's fingers, kidney vetch) to mention just two common plants. It is a solemn commentary on human morality and pessimism however that while only half a dozen or so plants and flowers are blessed with the name "angel", no less than sixty others have been saddled with the prefix "devil". Flower names like "witch bells", "witch milk" and the better known "witch hazel" remind us of the ancient link between evil spirits and plants. The greater celandine, which is known in Gloucestershire as "the devil's milk", is called the *Hexen Kraut* in Germany. The peculiar virtue of this plant lies in its effectiveness as a cure for warts.

When we attempt to rediscover some of the reasons for man's attitude to the plant world we find that flowers became credited with spiritual qualities as a by-product of the gradual growth of religious ideas over the centuries, a process which appears to have been universal. The plant, tree or flower was assumed to possess an indwelling spirit or soul which determined its growth and shaped its purpose as well as its bearing upon the welfare or otherwise of mankind. The rowan or mountain ash, for example, was supposed to possess the power to protect the home against witchcraft and similar evils; it was also employed as a magical charm to shield domestic cattle from sickness. Without doubt the scarlet berries of this particular tree were responsible for the supernatural awe with which it was regarded. From earliest times all blood-coloured berries have been considered life symbols in the same way that black has become symbolic of death and mourning.

The Irish have inherited a curious tradition to account for plants with poisonous berries. When the fairies were expelled from Heaven they apparently brought with them large numbers of plants which were destined to be of inestimable value to mankind. Satan, with his traditional guile, then complicated the situation by duplicating most of them with the result that only an individual highly skilled in the magical arts was able to distinguish between a poisonous plant and one with healing properties. This offers an explanation why even today country herbalists seem to have been influenced by supernatural considerations when distilling their herbal brews, muttering incantations of the rhythmic kind and stirring their cauldrons clockwise, this being the traditional ritual for linking human actions with the rotary movements of the sun.

The benign witchcraft of the herbalists embodied elements of vanished religious beliefs combined with much practical good sense. Its survival into modern times is a fitting testimonial of its value to the people.

We can understand the sense of the marvellous which was aroused by the floral world when we consider how mystifying the blooming of flowers must have appeared to primitive communities who had not the faintest conception of time as we know it.

Something of this awareness of the arcane is evident in the Irish ode to the laurustinus, a plant dedicated to St Faine whose day is January 1st:

> Whether the weather be snow or rain
> We are sure to see the flower of St Faine.
> Rain comes but seldom and often snow
> And yet the viburnum is sure to blow.

The opening and closing of the flower petals with almost clockwork precision must have further enhanced this sense of awe. One of the most remarkable of the so-called flower clocks – the Marvel of Peru – unfolds its petals regularly at four in the afternoon. And in our English countryside we have the yellow goat's beard opens its petals at four in the morning.

The Romanies and tramps who once roamed the countryside must have been the last of the rural population to employ flower clocks as timepieces, especially on overcast days when the sundial or old-fashioned church scratch-dial would have been useless.

Despite these romantic allusions to the past it is often easy for the twentieth-century flower lover to forget the harsh fact that our remote ancestors seem to have valued flowers largely as items of food. Apparently, some twenty thousand or so years ago, the bulbs of the narcissus and the hyacinth were appreciated solely for their vegetable properties by the plant gatherers who roamed the heathlands in quest of roots and herbs. As Daphne Barraclough puts it in her intriguing *A Flower-Lover's Miscellany*: "The gay dahlia meant nothing more in those days than its tubers provided valuable starchy food."

It is a little realized gastronomical fact that flowers (like vegetables) have provided dishes through the ages for the enjoyment of those with a taste for delicate viands. The guest at a medieval feast would have expected to find marigold petals as an ingredient of his soup, while his baronial host would very likely have offered him a stew of primroses. Meats, like venison, would have been garnished with marigolds, and yellow chrysanthemum petals seeped in salt water provided a delicate garnish for the fish dish. Salads were rendered even more palatable by the addition of such delicacies as the flowers and leaves of the nasturtium. Even today the conscientious cook in quest of variety will often turn to the old books of culinary delights for pleasing floral recipes.

In these repositories of domestic magic we find recipes for flower-scented sugars and aromatic vinegars; rose petal conserves may still be found in the pantries of old-fashioned country housewives, together with syrup of violets, pickled cowslips and candied rose petals. For the thirsty there is meadow-sweet beer, or even heather ale, which is one of the lost pleasures of the table.

Flowers are essential for the decoration of the festive board; indeed no dinner or luncheon table can be said to be properly "dressed" without them.

However, while proper reverence for flowers might serve as a guide to the level of sophistication in society, it can often become obsessional, as we find in the annals of classical antiquity where it is clear that this passion was carried to the extremes. The incredibly lavish suppers of Mark Antony and Cleopatra were held in salons garlanded with blossoms which were also heaped upon the floors to provide a superb carpet for the guests. The inordinately sensual Roman Emperor Nero was showered with rose petals by his attendants and his banqueting hall sprayed with perfumes as he entered it. During the feast itself rose petals cascaded down upon the heads of the guests from specially constructed apertures in the ceilings. According to an old writer, "even in the time of the Republic, people were not satisfied if the Falernian wine were not perfumed with roses."

Roman and Greek banqueting boards were decorated with incredible quantities of flowers which were expected to stimulate the hunger of the guests. To quote Xenophanes, the Greek poet: "the odour of flowers was deemed potent to arouse the fainting appetite."

Historians tell us that the Greeks were even more obsessive about flowers than their imitators the Romans, for "not only were they then, as now, the ornament of beauty, and of the altars of the gods, but the youths crowned themselves with them in the fêtes, the priest in religious ceremonies and the guests in convivial meetings." The Greeks had their own nymph of flowers named Chloris, who if not actually worshipped like Flora the Roman goddess of flowers, provided the supernatural element in Greek botany. Even in the sacrifices carried out in the temples flowers were given a central role, the priest being garlanded while the unhappy individual chosen for immolation had a farewell blossom placed in his hand.

> Thus the gay victim with fresh garlands crowned
> Pleased with the sacred pipes' enlivening sound,
> Through gazing crowds in solemn state proceeds
> And dressed in fatal pomp magnificently bleeds.

Flowers seem to have been integral with the ancient concept of the after-life, for even in the gloomy regions of the Elysian fields presided over by Pluto the vast plains were covered with asphodel. These particular flowers were planted by the Greeks and Romans on graves to symbolize eternal life.

The association of beautiful flowers with funerals has been continued into our own times; this tribute we pay to our dead, in the shape of floral wreaths, is a relic of a custom borrowed from the past. Originally funeral flowers represented a floral offering or alternatively a token sacrifice to the departed with the objective of reconciling them to their fates, perhaps to obviate any temptation they might have to return to their old homes as ghosts. Looked at from this aspect, the funeral wreath is no more than a magic circle specifically designed to enclose the dead soul. The ancient Egyptians went even further and crowned their dead with chaplets of flowers which served not only as a farewell gift but ensured for them a speedy journey to the other world.

Floral wreaths were strongly opposed by the church in the early years of Christianity because of their obviously pagan origins yet, as we have seen, the magic of flowers has proved stronger than papal edicts, and the floral wreath is now fully established as an orthodox symbol of death.

Earlier we mentioned the familiar trait of endowing forms of life other than our own with human attributes, and the idea of the indwelling soul which was at one time supposed to animate plants, flowers and trees. Although the older form of this belief is rarely evident in modern countries it lingers on here and there in legends of fairies and elves, the old-time elemental spirits of the woodlands.

In fact a great many common plants have been given fairy names, a well-known example being Fairy Gloves, the folk name of the foxglove, and it would be correct to assume from such cases that the belief in a fairy race closely involved the realm of plants and flowers.

Charles Skinner describes in fanciful terms in his *Myths and Legends of Flowers* how "the little people hid in flowers, made their cloaks of petals, their crowns of stamens, their darts of thorns, their cradles of lilies, their seats of fungi", and then makes the interesting comment: "They were the souls of flowers, mischievous when the flowers exhaled a poison; beneficent when the flowers were wholesome."

Fairies apparently sheltered in the anemone to escape from the thunderstorm and there they slept at night. Many had a protective role but could be expected to take revenge upon those who interfered in their affairs. One consequence of injuring the stitchwort was to be fairy led; that is, to be lured into some treacherous bog where the offender would be sucked down to death. However, anyone so endangered could find his way home again by the simple expedient of turning his coat inside out, which neutralized the fairy power.

It is strange that the same fairy tradition should have lingered so long in the flower kingdom although, admittedly, it is now almost entirely confined to very young children; however, from the fact that the old stories continue to be told, it can perhaps be assumed that they retain the affections of the older generation.

In fact, the word "fairy" only acquired its present connotation in the post-medieval period; previously "elf" had been used instead. This will no doubt explain why so many plants became associated in one way or another with elves as well as fairies in popular lore. Later the terms elf and fairy became interchangeable.

The elves belonged to a diminutive race of elemental spirits which haunted the forests of ancient Germany and constituted a kind of link between mankind and the spirit world. By the seventeenth century beliefs had changed somewhat and the fairy kingdom was presumed to occupy a half-way position between mankind and the angels. By and large the entire race of fairyland seems to have been associated with the vegetable kingdom in one way or another.

Some elves resided in trees, the oak being a favourite of theirs, but many took the flowers under their protection, especially the rose. The cowslip was another favourite, hence Shakespeare's lines from *The Tempest*:

> Where the bee sucks, there suck I
> In a cowslip's bell I lie;

It will be remembered also that in *A Midsummer-Night's Dream* Puck is compelled by Oberon to procure for him a pansy which had power to make a "man or woman madly dote/Upon the next live creature that it sees."

Yellow flowers seem to have been loathed by the fairy kingdom despite the deep affection they felt for most other blossoms. This was possibly due to the fact that yellow was the ancient symbol of sickness and later became the recognized livery of the devil.

To acquire the ability to see fairies one has only to prepare a concoction of distilled flowers incorporating rose-water, marigold water and magical herbs. Wild thyme must then be added and the whole left to settle for three days in sunlight. If dabbed upon the eyes or used regularly as an eye lotion it opens the windows of the fairy kingdom to the magically-minded botanist. Nevertheless, it might be unwise to put this charm to the test. The fairies themselves could be transported wherever they wilt by riding on a ragwort, known to countryfolk as "the fairies' horse". Similarly a cabbage stalk provided an aerial steed; or a fern or a blade of grass. The fairy kingdom was guarded against prying eyes by secret doorways overgrown with flowers which opened to the cowslip, sometimes known as the "key flower".

In Northern Europe rose gardens lay under the powerful protection of Laurin, a dwarf king who was "lord of the roses" and

Elfin Flowers

lived within a fairy hill. He derived his authority from a magic cap, a girdle and a ring.

> Four portals to the garden lead and when the gates are closed
> No living soul dare touch a rose, 'gainst his strict command
> opposed.

Laurin, whose subterranean abode was illuminated by precious stones, captured Kunhild, the spirit of Summer, and made her his prisoner. In this way the fairy folk brought Winter into the world.

CHAPTER TWO

Planting and Moon Magic

Throughout the world the planting of the seed has always been accompanied by magical ceremonies whether the plant happened to be a flower, a herb or a tree. Behind this ceremony there slumbers even today the remnant of a very old belief which holds it possible, by human action or ritual, to influence favourably the health and growth of the crops. Many authors have written on this subject, including Sir James Frazer who described in his book *The Golden Bough* how in old-time Europe the flax-sower believed that by taking long strides while he planted his seeds the growth of the plant could be accelerated. In Sumatra the women who sowed the rice crop let their long hair hang down freely, believing that by so doing the stalks would grow correspondingly longer.

Examples of this curious attitude are legion, and even in Britain there lingered on until comparatively recent times a number of rites which were influenced by religion and magic. For example, the belief that beans should be sown on saints' days if they are to prosper, although it is possible that seasonal climatic conditions may sometimes have influenced the choice, hence the old saying well known to gardeners:

> Sow beans and peas on David and Chad
> Whether the weather be good or bad.

The end of the period for sowing was defined by yet another curious jingle:

Be it weal or be it woe
Beans should blow before May go.

Incidentally, there once existed a firm belief that the souls of the dead made their homes in the flowers of the broad bean, which is a possible indication that when cultivators finally emancipated themselves from the belief in the flower fairy the soul took its place in the folklore of flowers.

In rural Hertfordshire it is still believed that potatoes, peas and parsley have to be planted on Good Friday afternoon if they are to prosper. Parsley was once expected to "go seven times to the Devil" before it emerged from the soil, this superstition possibly arising because it germinates very slowly. It is, in fact, supposed to be unlucky to make a present of parsley roots to a friend, and it is psychically dangerous to transplant it. This tradition arose from the custom among the ancient Greeks of strewing graves with parsley flowers. At one time those on the point of death were described as "being in need of parsley".

There still exists among countryfolk a strong aversion to planting seeds of any kind on Friday the thirteenth, but this is no more than a variant of a superstition which applies to all operations demanding an element of luck for their success.

Incantations and words of power were once inseparable from agricultural operations, and it was no doubt for this very reason that an old Essex woman came under suspicion of witchcraft in the eighteenth century after being heard muttering a few verses of doggerel whilst watering her flowers. The barbaric mob who half-drowned her in an attempt to verify their suspicions that she had sold her soul to the Devil, would have had their hands full today for talking to flowers has become a universally accepted method of "making one's garden grow". Indeed, Lyle Watson, the American scientific writer, declares that incantations have a powerful influence on plant growth. In his book *Supernature* he points out that geraniums have been known to grow faster and taller to the accompaniment of classical music.

It is possible to detect from the use of incantations by gardeners during seed planting a technique for encouraging crop growth by rhythmic vibrations which are picked up by the sensitive organs of the plant.

Those to whom magic is still an important factor in everyday life are convinced that dancing ensures success in agricultural operations. Intricate movements in imitation of the sun's passage across the heavens have been devised to invoke the benevolent powers of nature and keep at bay the evil which threatens the living seed. There were also dances to induce rainfall; the ancient Mexicans and North American Indians held festivals which were designed to invoke the supernatural powers to offset the possibility of drought.

Many European folk dances were performed in the early part of the year to ensure fertility in the newly planted crops, most of them involving "magical" gestures.

There were places in the North American farmlands where the pioneer, newly arrived from the superstitious Old World carried out planting customs which must have originated in the childhood of the human race, for he would strip his wife naked and harness her to his plough when the first furrows were cut.

Although many of the ancient planting rituals have ceased to be observed, even among the so-called backward races, special ceremonies are performed occasionally by foresters at the planting of trees, including the burial of a copper coin in the earth.

The well-known ritual in which a tree is planted to commemorate an important occasion such as a coronation can be traced back for many thousands of years. There is a reference in the Old Testament (Genesis) to a ceremony when Abraham planted a grove in Beersheba. In countries like Norway it is customary to plant a tree to commemorate the birth of a baby, and there is an associated superstition which declares that if the tree falls prematurely some disaster will affect either the individual or his home.

> If the bough break, the baby will fall
> And down will come cradle and baby and all.

Trees were dedicated, with special ceremonies, by ancient peoples to their gods. Some trees originated as human beings, as in the legend of the miraculous transformation of Daphne into a laurel when she sought to escape from the overtures of the god Apollo. Tree nymphs known as dryads were so closely involved with the life of the tree that they suffered intense agonies if it was cut, and died when it was felled.

Trees of every kind have always been associated with the

supernatural, largely because they belong to a realm of nature closely involved with the gods. Apart from the guardian trees already mentioned, there was a dragon or elsbeer tree (otherwise the Elder) which provided the branches which were suspended outside houses on Walpurgis-night, the eve of May 1st, when, according to popular German superstition, witches met and held revels with the Devil. In Africa and Malaya certain trees were supposed to be dedicated to the Devil, and to these the maladies of human beings were ritually transferred by the witch doctor or tribal healer.

Abode trees were the arboreal homes of the elves and, strange to relate, there were also speaking trees. The Bushmen of South Africa believed that a woman's glance had the power to transform a man into a tree which then spoke with a human voice. There were countries where corpses were placed in the branches of funeral trees, the ground beneath becoming strewn with human bones.

The legendary lore of trees is extensive and takes us perhaps too far from our principal theme which is mainly concerned with gardening lore. Nevertheless, even our domesticated trees have their magical tale to tell. In Denmark for example the cherry had sinister associations since demons were known to lurk among its branches. In Korea one can exorcize a tree which has been taken over by demons by waving a magic wand cut from a peach tree.

One need say no more to illustrate the mysterious world in which mankind dwelt for thousands of years until the jungles were cut down and the tree demons exorcized from the environment. It was a world in which mankind walked alone, conscious that from behind the tree-trunks there were watching eyes; at such times one was aware of forces beyond the range of understanding.

The large number of moon superstitions and myths which are still current are a reminder that for untold centuries it was taken for granted that the heavenly bodies exerted a supernatural influence upon the lives of human beings and the world in which they lived. It is still thought unlucky to point at the new moon when seeing it for the first time. Not so long ago it was customary to raise one's hat, or curtsey. In the West Country the new moon was occasionally greeted with the poetical invocation:

New moon, new moon, first time I've seen thee,
I hope before the week be out I'll have something
given me.

The moon influenced both birth and death. A child born when the moon was waning would be unlucky all its life. Should a death take place at the time of the new moon further deaths could be anticipated in the family. However, the most widely accepted superstitions were related to the influence of the moon on vegetation.

The majority of gardeners will be familiar with certain old-fashioned notions suggesting that the moon has an important influence upon flowers and vegetables and that planting should be carried out with this fact in mind.

Even scientific flower growers have been known to plan their activities in accordance with the principles of moon magic. There is a strong belief that potatoes must be planted in the "dark of the moon", and if possible on Good Friday when the holy powers are strongest. Peas, on the other hand, should be sown in the "light of the moon". Between the first quarter and the full moon is the time for planting root crops, but leafy plants should be left until the "turn" of the lunar month when the moon begins to wane.

Among the Amish people of Pennsylvania even the placing of the fence posts separating their plots is regulated according to the phases of the moon.

There is a hint of moon magic in Deuteronomy in the phrase, "precious things are put forth by the moon, but precious fruits by the sun", which suggests that while the sun is a luminary with the life-giving rays, his pale sister the moon has jurisdiction over the growth of plant life.

Among many old books on the subject one of the most interesting was *The Garden Of Eden* published in 1600 which urged cultivators to take into consideration the phases of moon when planning a flower garden. According to this work single flowers like the gillyflower and the tulip can be made to double if they are transplanted three days after the full moon. *The Expert Gardener*, a seventeenth-century work which drew upon the experiences of Continental gardeners, counselled its readers to "sow and replant all manner of seeds in accordance with the phases of the moon", and in a series of brief instructions reminded them that violets, rosemary and lavender must be sown when the moon is new, and wallflowers when it is old. Another work, *The English Gardener*, published later in the seventeenth century, versifies its gardening guidance thus:

> If you with flowers would stick the pregnant earth
> Mark well the moon propitious to their birth,
> For earth the silent midnight queen obeys
> And waits her course, who clad in silver rays
> The eternal round of time and seasons guides. . . .

John Evelyn, the seventeenth-century diarist, strongly doubted the influence of the moon upon cultivation. He advanced the revolutionary viewpoint in a famous book *Sylva, or a Discourse of Forest Trees*, published in 1662. This strongly castigated gardeners of the "muck and magic" doctrine: "Those nice and hypercritical punctillos which some astrologers and such as peruse these rules and seem to oblige our gardeners too as if all forsooth were lost and our pains to no purpose unless the sowing and the planting, the cutting and the pruning were performed at such and such an exact minute of the moon."

When Evelyn wrote these words the breeze of science was just beginning to stir the weeds of long established precept governing every area of belief. The influence of astrology upon cultivation and gardening was extremely strong throughout the seventeenth century, but it should be remembered that the astrologers were the scientists of their day and their guidance was sought in every conceivable situation whether it was planning a wedding, a military campaign or a plantation. With the eighteenth century came scientific gardening and the rapid and almost complete eclipse of the star-gazing fraternity.

A great deal of the mystical approach to gardening was an inheritance from classical times when every department of life had its deity who was honoured in song and dance by worshippers who accepted its supremacy over the fate of mankind. The rural deities, or gods of the woods, included Pan, Sylvanus, the Fauni, Satyri, Silenus, Priapus, Aristaeus and Terminus.

Pan was a bearded figure with a ruddy face, horns, hairy thighs, a tail and the hooves of a goat.

Sylvanus, who presided over woodlands had, like Pan, the feet of a goat and a human face, but was much smaller.

Silenus was old, short and corpulent with a bald head, flat nose and elongated ears. A dedicated wine bibber, he was usually depicted in a drunken state, endeavouring to maintain a precarious balance on the back of an ass. His companions were the Satyrs, who when they grew old were known as Sileni Fauni.

Priapus, offspring of Venus and Bacchus, god of wine, was god of gardens and is represented carrying a sickle and crowned with herbs.

Aristaeus was the first to discover olive oil and the use of honey.

Terminus, the deity who governed boundaries, was held in great honour by the Romans. His effigy took the form of a square stone, or a shaped log which was used to mark the boundaries of estates. The last day of the year was celebrated in his honour.

Flora, the goddess of flowers, was originally named Chloris. She was wife to Zephyrus, the west wind, and their union symbolized that "the natural heat of the plant must be united with the gentlest wind to bring it to perfection."

Vertumnus was the Roman god of orchards.

Pomona, from *pomum*, an apple (and fruit in general), presided over the fruits of plants and trees.

Dryads and Hamadryads, although wood nymphs, were included among the rural deities.

In order to appreciate fully the intense mystical reverence felt by the old-style husbandman for the procreative powers in nature one turns to Ceres, the corn goddess, from whom we obtain the word "cereal". Ceres is represented in ancient art as a tall majestic woman with corn-coloured hair crowned with ears of corn. She carries in her right hand poppies and wheat, and in her left a lighted torch.

She was also the goddess of fruits and is credited with having first taught mankind the arts of husbandry. From the beginnings, therefore, we see how closely cultivation was associated with religious and mystical ideas.

Ceres' favourite daughter Proserpine was carried off into the underworld by the god Pluto, but later restored to her mother, with whom she dwelt half the year in Heaven, the other half year being spent in the underworld. In this fable Ceres represents the earth and Proserpine the seed which was buried in the ground during winter but in summer time basked in the light of the life-giving sun.

The corn festival, as carried out in wheat-growing lands, was centred around the corn dolly which represented Ceres, the ancient corn goddess. The corn dolly, a small figurine plaited by the oldest farm worker in the last stook of corn as it stood in the harvest field, was cut with a great deal of ceremony and taken into the farmhouse where it was retained until the following harvest. It was then replaced by a dolly from the new crop. The corn dolly, or kern baby as it is sometimes called, was believed to bring good fortune to the farmhouse where it was kept suspended above the hearth. The traditional corn dolly no longer graces the hearth, but the idea survives in the church Harvest Festival during which the font is decorated with wheat, fruit and flowers.

A curious tradition has grown up around modern harvest dolls plaited by rural groups and Women's Institutes, taking the form of the superstition that any woman who is presented with a corn dolly will have a baby during the following year.

Even the gathering of the flower harvest was at one time accompanied by general rejoicing stimulated by a feeling of thanksgiving for the successful fulfilment of a year's labours. Most cultivators celebrated the occasion with feasts accompanied by singing and dancing.

There was much rejoicing at the gathering of the lavender harvest in nineteenth-century England, especially in Hertfordshire and at Mitcham in Surrey, a county renowned for its lavender where the last of the harvest was bunched and tied to the farm cart and later burned in the field. The word "lavender" is derived from the Latin verb *lavare* – to wash – for the flower was once extensively used for the perfuming of baths. In Spain and Portugal the harvesting was carried out with some apprehension because of the belief that the asp, one of the most dangerous types of viper, made its home in the lavender beds. The Tuscans used lavender as a protective charm against the evil eye and witchcraft. In North Africa wives wore it as an amulet to protect themselves from wife-beating husbands.

Harvest ceremonies were inspired by the desire to give thanks to the god or goddess who presided over the crops and brought them to fruition. These celebrations have long since lost their

Moon Magic

pagan characteristics in Christian countries where they have been replaced by days of religious observance. The same idea is embodied in the celebration of Thanksgiving in the United States and Canada.

Overshadowing the gathering of the first flower of the season there were always a number of doleful superstitions to be borne in mind. The snowdrop, which is also known as February Fair Maid, is associated with death due to the belief that the "flowers wear shrouds", an allusion to the peculiar formation of the petals. It is supposed to be ominous if the first snowdrop of the season be brought into the home. In some places in the British Isles it is also considered unlucky to bring the first daffodil indoors since this beautiful spring flower is associated with doom and disaster. The poet Homer provided a clue to the mystery when he wrote, "although this flower delighted Heaven and earth by its odour and beauty, yet at the same time it produces stupor, madness and even death . . ." In ancient Greece a crown of narcissi was placed upon the heads of corpses before burial, which is no doubt the source of the sad superstition.

Another mournful tradition is associated with the bean flower. The Romans held a festival of the dead in the month of May in which the populace threw black beans onto the graves of their loved ones, with the result that the bean flower continues to be contaminated with unhappiness. To dream of bean flowers is an omen of disaster, arising from the belief among country folk that they contained the souls of the dead. In mining districts there was a superstition that accidents occurred more frequently when the bean was in flower than at any other season of the year.

CHAPTER THREE

Legends, Symbols, and Superstition

As creative people are aware, one of the strongest factors influencing art and poetry is the beauty and mystery of the realm of nature. Trees, plants and flowers have provided inspiration for artists past and present. The garlands, chaplets and wreaths used on ceremonial occasions are one aspect of floral artistry, as is the modern cult of flower arrangement which is largely designed for pleasure or display.

To the minds of our ancestors, however, the significance of a particular flower meant much more than the aesthetic pleasures it aroused. Flowers were employed from earliest times as symbols to express in a concise fashion an abstraction or idea. When a medieval lady was addressed by her knight-errant as his "rose", the intention was not to suggest that she had feet of clay, but to convey to the damsel that she was an exotically perfumed goddess of love, a delight to the eye, whose presence hallowed the world in which she walked. To be described as a weed is an obvious expression of contempt.

To the symbolist a single rose signifies perfection, being emblematic of "the heart of mystic centre of being". For this reason the rose was adopted by poets and dreamers to symbolize all that was ideal, serving as the emblem of Venus and the *Paradiso* of Dante. The symbolic values are derived from the number of the petals as well as the colours. To ancient magicians the rose had a meaning known only to adepts of the secret arts: a seven-petalled rose, for example, represented the seven degrees of absolute perfection, and an eight-petalled one regeneration or rebirth.

The realm of flowers provided allegories suitable for every artistic situation, as we find in Keats' lines:

> No flower amid the garden fairer grows
> Than the sweet lily, of the lowly vale
> The Queen of flowers

and Brown's:

> The gentle daisy with her silver crown
> Worn in the breast of many a shepherd lass.

Surrounded as they were by flowers, our forefathers drew moral lessons from the garden scene, many of which will be familiar to readers.

The life of a flower is brief, and this influenced poets, artists and magicians who employed it as a self-evident symbol of transience, with the wider message to seize the hour before it passes. "Gather ye rosebuds while ye may," says Herrick, "Old Time is still a-flying . . ." On the other hand, the concept of eternity finds expression in the English proverb: "An elder stake and a blackthorn hedge will make a hedge to last forever."

The mystery of growth combined with the supernatural qualities which were so long associated with flowers, and their aesthetic appeal, made them ideal religious symbols. In ancient Egypt the lotus became the symbol of new life, and in Europe was equated like the rose with the mystical centre or heart of things. Without delving too deeply into the occultism of the East we find the lotus symbolizing the mystic dwelling place of Brahma, the visible manifestation of his occult powers. In India it is depicted growing from the navel of the god Vishnu, and represents the universe stemming from a "central sun".

The language of ideas, which is more perfectly expressed by flowers than by any other existing thing, rendered them a perfect medium for religious expression in art.

In Christian art, which is far more meaningful to the European flower-lover, we find special values ascribed to flowers associ-

Lotus Flower

ated with God, the Trinity and above all the Virgin Mary. The floral art of the great masters is based entirely upon the religious meanings of the various flowers portrayed, its object being to express the truths concealed within the great mysteries. Formal religion can never be more than a veil behind which great truths serve as lights to illuminate the hearts and minds of true initiates. Flowers were adopted as Christian symbols because they could be made to express explicitly and implicitly certain aspects of God which were not communicable by words. The association of flowers with the Church goes back to its days of torment and trial during the persecutions in ancient Rome when floral emblems were utilized by worshippers as a form of communication when the need for secrecy was essential. When a lily is held in the hand of the Virgin it is her attribute, but if it appears alone it is her emblem; when it represents the concept of purity it becomes her symbol. In medieval times a picture depicting Christ demanded no specific symbolic expression. An angel bearing an olive branch in his hand was clearly recognizable to all Christians as a peacemaker. It is to the Renaissance that we owe the inclusion of flowers and fruit in religious art.

Giocachino di Flo Fiore who is regarded by many as the spiritual father of the Franciscan principle, held that all life was divided into three creative phases, the first witnessing the birth of the stars, the second the first dawn, and the third the daylight glory, each being reflected in a particular style of floral creation. The first was the age of nettles, the second that of the rose, and the third the age of the lily. The lily was originally employed by Christian artists as an emblem to illustrate the marvels of Paradise, but later became established as the symbol of purity to be replaced by in time the rose as the emblem of heavenly delights.

There has been, as we have seen, a constant reassessment of the meanings of flowers in art. From the twelfth century onwards, for example, the lily became the emblem of the Virgin and the saints, the only flower to rival it in purity being the iris which is known as the Sword Lily by the Germans because of its sword-shaped leaves. In France this flower is identifiable with the fleur-de-lis. The trefoil or shamrock, representing the Holy Trinity, was used by St Patrick to illustrate to the pagan Irish the meaning of the True Godhead. Michelangelo, who only rarely

Christian Emblems

employed symbolic details, used the trefoil in his masterpiece, "The Holy Family".

The daisy is another flower which enjoys a prominent place in religious art, and also the marguerite and the sunflower which are sun symbols, as are the white and yellow chrysanthemum.

Those who employed flower symbolism for the presentation of their religious concepts could find biblical authority in the Song of Solomon which introduced such delightful metaphors as "a lily among thorns", "the flower of the fields" and "a rose of Sharon".

The rose, long an outcast among Christians as a flower originally associated with Venus, goddess of carnal love, was gradually accepted as an emblem of martyrdom and virginity, divine love and heavenly joy.

Many flowers were featured in representation of the garden of Heaven of the older paintings, the rose, the lily and the pink among well-known examples. The pink was depicted as the flower of holy love, the flowering strawberry righteousness, while the jasmine, known as the star of divine hope, was associated with the Madonna.

Not only did people once believe in the existence of flowers of virtue – in the religious sense – but also in their opposites, flowers of evil which were used in black magic. These included the cyclamen, a favourite of necromancers who manufactured love philtres, and the poppy, which was an emblem of sloth and the forbidden rites of pagan love. "Evil" blossoms appear but rarely in religious art, for Christian iconography limited itself to flowers and plants which the theologians decreed to be attributes of the divine and holy.

In England the national feeling for flowers was demonstrated in architectural detail and in the art of the miniaturists, executed by the medieval monks, a tradition which died out with the end of monasticism only to be revived in the middle of the nineteenth century under the influence of the Pre-Raphaelite Brotherhood. One of these, George Frederick Watts, who has been described as the greatest of nineteenth-century religious mystics, drew upon the allegory of flowers extensively in his paintings, although the symbolism he employed was largely his own and not that of the mystical and religious artists of earlier ages.

Fruit also had an important role in Christian art. In Sienna Cathedral we find fruit carved in stone garlands set around the circular windows. The Florentines enclosed their Madonnas within frames of golden fruit, an apt choice for these symbols of joy, peace and love, the true fruits of the Holy Spirit. When wreathed around the image of a saint, fruit represents deeds of righteousness; looped above his head it is his crown of victory.

In artistic works the fruit of the Tree of Knowledge was not invariably the apple, for the fig, the quince and the pear appear among the lures which tempted Eve and led to the banishment of mankind from that blissful if mythical Garden of Eden.

Flowers are popular in architectural decoration, especially the vine, the poppy, the sunflower, palm sprays, ivy, oak, olive, laurel, bay, and frequently roses and ivy leaves combined. The heraldic interpretation of the iris is the fleur-de-lis in all its varied forms, and is employed in Spanish art as the symbol of the Immaculate Conception. In ancient times the rose was embossed on the ceilings of banqueting halls as a symbol of silence, a gentle reminder that words spoken beneath it were confidential, i.e. *sub rosa* – under the rose.

The religious attitude towards art is ideally expressed by a member of the Franciscan order who wrote: "Mindful of the festival which our church prescribes, I have sought to make these objects of floral nature the timepieces of my religious calendar." He indicated to his readers how the blossoming of the various flowers corresponded to the different festivals of his church: "Thus I can light a taper to our Virgin Mother on the blowing of the white snowdrop . . . the ladies smock and the daffodil remind me of the Annunciation, the blue harebell of the Festival of St George . . ." and he concludes: ". . . Michaelmas Martinmas Holy Rood and Christmas all have their appropriate decorations."

The Christmas festival witnesses the decoration of our churches with flowers, holly, otherwise the holy tree, rosemary, laurel and bay. The mistletoe was a prohibited plant because of its historical connection with the Druids, while ivy was restricted to the outer passages of the building. Christmas, which has been called "The Festival of Festivals", saw also the decoration of the church interior with evergreens as symbols of eternal life and also in fulfilment of the commands of God uttered through the mouth of the prophet Isaiah: "The glory of Lebanon shall come unto thee, the fir tree, the pine tree and the box together to beautify the place of my sanctuary and I will make the place of my feet glorious."

The heyday of floral decoration in our churches occurred immediately following the Reformation. Apparently the devastation carried out by the Protestant reformers in the days of Edward VI stripped the churches of their splendid candle-lit monuments and shrines, and to compensate partially for this situation flowers were introduced into churches by the Elizabethans. Many sixteenth- and seventeenth-century account books include entries of expenditure on flowers in place of the earlier payments for candle wax.

The iconoclastic hand struck again, this time at the floral decoration of churches during the Puritan upsurge of the seventeenth century. However, there was a revival of floral art in churches at a later period. William Andrews refers to this happy situation in his *Church Treasury* published in 1898: "The ceremonial use of flowers has of recent years greatly revived. In village, town and city the ancient or modern sanctuary may be seen at frequent intervals from New Year to Christmas brightened with blossoms or decorated with evergreens while in many cases the altar is daily adorned with fresh flowers whenever they can be obtained. . . . It has been well said that of all customs that of adorning the 'Holy Place of the Tabernacle of the most High' with flowers and wreaths at Christmas and other festivals of the Christian year speaks of the fervent love of our ancestors more strongly than any other."

A curious religious custom, now almost forgotten, took the form of a Flower Sermon, during which all the worshippers carried flowers. As late as 1894 these sermons were preached annually in country churches throughout the land, every member of the congregation laying a bunch of flowers on the altar.

The idea of sacrifice has always been dear to the human heart, and is explained by the literal meaning of the word which is "to make sacred". Sacrifice represents in practical terms an attempt to win the favour of a god, and above all to express thanksgiving, sometimes in the form of a flower or flowers. The dedication of particular flowers, plants and trees to gods is another very ancient and beautiful custom and older by far than the Christian ritual. In classical religion every deity had its individual sphere of influence which dictated the kind of favour sought by the worshipper, in return for the flower that he offered.

Flower Offering	*God*	*Spiritual Domain*
Alder	Neptune	The sea
Apple	Venus	Love
Ash	Mars	War
Bay	Apollo	The sun
Beech	Jupiter-Ammon	Lord of Heaven and Prince of Light
Cypress	Pluto	Ruler of the Infernal Regions
Heliotrope	Phoebus Apollo	God of the Sun
Iris and Lily	Juno	Goddess of the Sun
Myrtle	Venus and Mars	Love/War
Narcissus	Ceres, Pluto and Proserpine	Mother Earth, Queen of the Infernal Regions
Pink	Jupiter	Lord of Heaven
Poppy	Ceres, Diana and Somnus	Mother Earth, Love/Sleep
Rose	Venus	Love

In the mythology of the Teutons and Scandinavians we find the rose is a sacred flower dedicated to Hulda, the Germanic goddess of marriage. Even the days of the week are allocated to the various gods each of whom is endowed with an appropriate floral emblem.

Day	*Emblem*	*Dedication*
Sunday	Sunflower	Day of the Sun
Monday	Daisy	Day of the Moon
Tuesday	March Violet	Day of Tyr, God of War

Day	*Emblem*	*Decoration*
Wednesday	Geranium	Day of Odin
Thursday	Monkshood	Day of Thor, God of Thunder
Friday	Polipodium	Day of Freya or Frigga
Saturday	Flowers/Fruit	Day of Saturn, God of Harvests and Time

It is but a step removed from the propitiation of gods with floral offerings to the attempts that were once made to communicate with the realm of the dead through the symbolism of flowers. There is actually a type of spiritualist seance where a flower is handed by the sitter to the medium. By holding this in the hand the medium can make contact with the psychic influence or spirit entity associated with the sitter, and set up a sympathetic relationship between the dead and the living. Again, in studying the importance of flower symbolism in dreams we enter an area of the supernatural which arouses intense interest among every type of person.

All students of the occult will be conscious of the immense importance of dreams, a fact recognized by seers from earliest times. The ancients believed that dreams were either expressions of the divine will or, alternatively, communications from the world of spirits, their meanings being capable of interpretation by diviners and magicians. To an ancient Egyptian dreams were inspired by the goddess Isis. The Greeks believed that dreams passed through one of the two gates guarding the Palace of Dreams: prophetic dreams entered and left this palace via a gate of transparent horn, and deceptive dreams via a gate of ivory.

The Hebrews held that the Lord expressed His will through the medium of dreams.

The Finnish Ugrics called the dream the Ort or shadow which wandered afar to assemble truths which were later interpreted by the dreamer. There was a clear-cut difference, however, between dreams and visions; the former occurred during sleep whereas the latter were seen in times of wakefulness. Incidentally, a dream which takes place immediately before dawn can be expected to come true.

There were five classes of dreams: the immediate vision; the revelation which occurred between sleeping and waking; the dream arising from suggestion; the ordinary dream; and lastly the type of divine apparition or revelation as experienced by the Magi of the East, which could be described as a vision.

The ancient art of dream interpretation, known as oneiromancy, is one of the most fascinating of all the occult sciences practised today. As a legacy from the magical past we have been bequeathed curious books of dream lore which discuss the various flowers and their symbolic meanings to the dreamer.

Flower	*Dream Meaning*
Almond	Luck in the home
Aster	Pleasurable recreations
Blossom	Happiness and good luck
Bouquet	Unsuspected love or romance lies ahead
Clover	Prosperity, love and happiness
Columbine	A happy adventure
Cowslip	Unexpected luck
Crocus	A fresh start
Cypress	Death
Daffodil	Love and happiness
Dahlia	A change for the better
Daisy	A birth
Edelweiss	Your lover is faithful
Evergreens	Good luck
Ferns	If growing satisfactorily – a good sign If trampled down – a sinister omen
Fir tree	Business problems face you / A loyal friend
Flowers generally	Picking flowers – happiness A bunch of flowers – a wedding Dropping flowers – disappointment
Forget-me-not	You are loved
Foxglove	You are lucky in love
Geraniums	A change of interests
Gorse	An opportunity is coming your way
Harebell	True love
Heather (White)	Good luck
Holly	Quarrels
Honeysuckle	Change of address
Hyacinth	Restoration of health

Flower	*Dream Meaning*
Ivy	True love
Jasmine	Romance
Laurel	You can expect a legacy
Lavender	A reunion
Leaves	Green – good luck Withered – treachery and sorrow
Lilac	Happy friendships
Lily	You stand alone
Lime flowers	Love
Marigold	You will do well
Meadow flowers	You will be lucky in love
Mignonette	Happiness ahead
Mistletoe	Take great care in love matters
Mowing	Business prospects will improve
Myrtle	You will shortly receive a proposal
Nettles	Good luck
Oak	Good health
Orange blossom	A wedding
Pansy	Contentment
Passion-flower	Loss of a lover
Peony	Worry
Pinks	A happy gathering of friends
Plants (in general)	Good health
Rhododendron	Happiness in the family
Rose	Love is on its way
Rosemary	Reunion
Shamrock	Expect a visitor from the past
Trees	Good health
Tulip	A secret romance
Violet	Young love
Water lily	A hopeless ideal
Weeds	Tidy up your life
Wreath	A contest

When considering the curious influence flowers exert upon the mind and their role in ritual, magic and art, one should not disregard two other aspects, colour and scent.

In discussing colour, we find that in bygone ages each of the chief colours had its own psychic and social value. Purple, a royal colour, was worn by the Roman Emperors. The gold with which buildings were so splendidly decorated was supposed to represent the rays of the sun. Red was the colour of blood and therefore the symbol of nobility, heroism and warfare. Blue was dedicated to Jupiter and was emblematic of water and the heavens above (temple ceilings were often painted blue to symbolize the heavenly vault). Yellow and gold were easily recognizable symbols of the sun, their meanings being power and wealth. White was a moon colour and green one of the emblems of the goddess Venus and also of vegetation. Black was the colour of winter, of earth without life.

Colour in the world around us and in the garden is of immense psychological importance; as Matthew Luckiesh observes in his fascinating work on colour: "Nature's palette is loaded with countless primary, secondary and tertiary colours and the contents are lavished with endless variety and unceasing energy."

This writer goes on to discuss our attitudes to flowers. Red, he points out, is appealing in flowers and fruit. Yellow is an unpopular colour, although "we react quite oppositely to dandelions on the lawn than we do to marigolds in the garden". However, he reminds us that the sun is "painted" yellow orange. Blue flowers, it appears, are less popular than those with warmer colours; the colour is dignified but cold, like the sky. Green, he insists, is a most satisfying colour for it is restful and neutral, a tranquillizer.

People quite unconcerned with the mystical characteristics of flowers or the intricacies of flower symbolism will be aware of a number of flower superstitions which crop up in daily life. There are blossoms which are harbingers of good luck, while others bring misfortune to all who handle them, but the great majority of flowers with mystical meanings convey messages relating to the future, although often of a most ominous kind. These communications are not to be confused with dreams which were discussed earlier. Whatever one's attitude to the supernatural might be, there is undoubtedly a great deal of interesting lore to be found in a study of flower superstitions. Indeed, they provide an insight into old-fashioned ways of thought – for many of the superstitions are centuries old.

In the following alphabetical list of well-known flowers – wild as well as domestic – we find reflected ideas which are both picturesque and informative and, it is hoped, amusing to the present generation of cultivators and those interested in folk medicine.

Agrimony was once regarded as an effective antidote for snake bites; and when bundled with rue, broom, maidenhair and ground ivy it enabled the one who carried it to recognize witches on sight. It acquired some of its supernatural qualities from the myth of Mithrides, King of Pontus, a skilled botanist who used agrimony to counteract poisons.

Anemone, or windflower, derived its name from the legend that it sprang from the blood of Adonis, the favourite lover of Venus. In ancient times the first anemone of the season was credited with healing powers. It was necessary to chant, "I gather these for a remedy against disease", and the flower was then wrapped in a scarlet cloth and tied to the arm of the sick person. This remedy is mentioned in an old English ballad:

> The first Spring-blown Anemone, she in his doublet wove
> To keep him safe from pestilence wherever he should rove.

Bachelor's Buttons. These flowers derived their name from their resemblance to buttons. They include the double red campion, the white campion and the crowfoot. The flower should be carried in the pocket and if it fades it is a sign that your love-life is threatened with disappointment.

Buttercup, so named because it formed the first link in the chain of life which finally ends up as butter and cream, with the humble cow as intermediary. For some unknown reason there exists the belief that smelling a buttercup leads to madness. However, it was once believed that it provided an antidote for lunacy when suspended around the patient's neck at the waning of the moon.

Carnation or Gillyflower is one of the blossoms which grew in Paradise. It is one of the symbols of divine love and therefore a luck bringer.

Cornflower or Centaury is a well-known floral oracle for testing the strength of a lover's affections. All is well with the romance provided the vividness of the colour is maintained. The whole idea is summed up in the pretty lines from *Faust*:

Now gentle flower, I pray thee tell
If any lover loves me well.
So may the fall of the morning dew
Keep the sun from fading thy tender blue.

The superstition is based on the classical legend of Cyranus who loved cornflowers and was found dead in a cornfield, in a bed of cornflowers, wearing a robe of cornflower blue.

Daffodil or Narcissus. Because of the tradition that the Greek youth Narcissus pined to death from love of his own reflection, the flower which sprung from his body is associated with the superstition that it is unlucky to bring a single daffodil into the home. This is probably the source of the custom among the Greeks of including narcissi in funeral wreaths.

Dandelion is known as the "rustic oracle" because its petals regularly open at around 5 a.m. and close again at 8 p.m. Children blow the dandelion seed-heads to tell the time. If you wish to discover whether your lover is thinking of you, blow the seed-heads. If there remains a single seed attached to the stalk it is a sign that you are not forgotten.

Elecampane. This "wild sunflower" provided the basis of a medieval recipe for those stricken with diseases by the elves. Chewing the root is supposed to "fasten loose teeth" and prevent dental decay.

Forget-me-not, Coleridge's "Hope gentle gem" was one of the medieval key flowers which provided an "open Sesame" to secret caverns where buried treasures lay concealed. To take possession of your treasure the flower must be pressed against the mountainside and the cavern walls will immediately fly open.

Foxglove. This is one of the genuine fairy plants. In Wales foxgloves are known as "goblin's gloves". They are also called "witches' thimble" because of the ancient tradition that witches decorated their fingers with the larger flowers. Country children will be aware that the flower was worn as a glove by foxes when chicken hunting, to muffle their tread.

Garlic. Juvenal says: "Each clove of garlic has a sacred flower." Known in India as "the slayer of monsters", garlic was used by old-time German miners to protect themselves against the assaults of evil spirits. In South-Eastern Europe it provided one of the defences against vampires. Among the English garlic was known as "poor man's treacle" and was used as an antidote against poisoning. To dream of garlic is an omen of good luck.

Globe Flower. This is one of the magic flowers once associated with witches and trolls. In ancient times it also served as a decoration for the outside of houses during the month of June. By the Japanese it is known as Kerria, the herald of summer.

Gorse or whin – a perennial. This wasteland plant is a symbol of enduring affection which has given us the well-known saying – "When kissing is out of season, the gorse is out of bloom." Gorse flowers were once suspended over Irish and Welsh doorways on May Day Eve to keep witches from the house. According to an old Yorkshire tradition the souls of the dead travelled to the other world by way of "whinny moor".

Harebell. A symbol of "childhood sorrow", it is also known as the "Devil's bell" (the hare is a witch's familiar) and it is therefore supernaturally dangerous to pick. In Ireland it is called "pucca's (i.e. goblin) finger". It is also an emblem of the Virgin Mary and associated with St George:

> On St George's Day when the blue is worn
> The blue harebells the fields adorn.

Hawthorn. The hawthorn has been regarded as a tree of mystery from early times. During the Middle Ages and later its destruction brought supernatural punishment. Branches of flowering hawthorn were suspended above house doorways for luck, but to bring hawthorn blossom inside the house was always unlucky. The Bretons call the hawthorn the "fairy thorn" believing it to be the trysting place of the little people. The Romans declared it to be the tree upon which the goddess Cardea cast her spells, and used the flowers as protective emblems for their homes.

Heather or Heath. There is an old German tradition that red heather owes its colour to the blood of the heathens who were slain in battle by the Christians. Because of its rarity, white heather brings good luck to the finder.

Honesty (*Lunaria biennis*): This was a plant used in witches' brews because of its moon-shaped seed vessels. Hence Chaucer's lines:

And herbes coude I tell eke many on
As Egremaine, Valerian and Lunarie.

It also cured madness. There is an old tradition that purple honesty thrives where the gardener is an honest person.

Honeysuckle was so named because of the honey dew found therein. It is one of the blossoms given by devout French lovers to their sweethearts to symbolize their union. It is also a plant with remarkable healing powers and will charm away your boils. An old legend tells of a witch who treated the sick by passing them thrice through a green garland cut from this plant.

Lavender. This charming plant is for some mysterious reason associated with dilettantes and those with trivial personalities. However, it is also a luck-bringer when kept either inside or outside the house. In Spain and Portugal lavender was used as fuel for the anti-witch bonfires which were lit on St John's Eve.

Lily. Plant lilies in your garden and if superstition be true they will keep your house free of ghosts and similar undesirable intruders. To tread on a lily accidentally indicates that your lover is unfaithful.

Lily of the Valley is one of the symbols of humility and chastity due to its whiteness and also to the fact that the heads are bowed as if in mourning. There is a rather horrible superstition that he who plants lilies of the valley in his garden can expect to die within a twelvemonth.

Marigold. A sun emblem, and a favourite floral clock. As Shakespeare says: "The Marigold goes to bed with the sun. And with him rises, weeping."

Moss-rose. As the symbol of voluptuous love, this flower must be picked "at the fall of the dew" on Midsummer's Eve to test the constancy of spouse or lover. Should it change colour, the worst may be expected. Otherwise, take heart, all is well.

Orange blossom. When carried by a bride this well-known symbol of femininity and perfection provides a guarantee against childlessness in marriage. This superstition is based on the ancient tradition that the orange is a fertility plant. There is, however, a sinister side to the story for Italian witches pierce oranges with pins and secrete them in chimneys until their victims die.

Peony. An emblem of Spring and an antidote to evil. In the days when black magic was a daily terror, the peony was employed by countryfolk as an anti-witch charm.

Periwinkle. Because the Italians place garlands of periwinkles upon the coffins of dead children they have become known as "the flowers of death". However, they are also symbols of immortality and emblems of "tender recollections". According to Culpeper, the English herbalist: "The leaves of the periwinkle, if eaten by man and wife together, cause love between them," especially when mixed with earthworms, perhaps a fanciful allusion to the old saying, "Go into the garden and eat worms"!

Plants and flowers associated with mourning. It was once the custom to drape flower pots and the flowers they contained in black crêpe when the family was in mourning. Should this ritual be omitted the flowers would wither and die.

Poppy. The poppy symbolizes evanescent pleasures and is generally speaking an unlucky flower. In some districts the wild variety is regarded as too sinister to bring inside the house. There is also a children's superstition that looking into the heart of a poppy causes blindness and also ear-ache if held too close to the ears. The ill-repute of the red poppy must be due to the old belief that "its colour hints of blood". According to an English legend the poppy sprang out of the blood of a dragon. The poppies bestrewing the fields of Flanders of World War I illustrate further the connection between this pretty flower and death.

Primrose. It is unlucky to bring less than a bunch at a time into the home at any one time, especially when the hens are broody as this threatens the lives of the young birds. To bring a single primrose into the home will also threaten the occupants with sickness or death. This superstition is possibly based on the tradition connected with the youth Paralisos, from which the flower derived its name, who died of grief after the death of his beloved. If a primrose blooms in Winter it is an evil portent. In the Isle of Man the flower was left on the doorstep on May Day Eve to keep witches from the home. The primrose path, that road of pleasure without virtue, is one of the major routes to Hell.

Rose. A lucky flower and a Christian symbol of charity. If a bouquet of roses is accidentally scattered it is a sign of trouble ahead. Among the Germans "it was customary to throw rose leaves onto a coal fire as a means of ensuring good luck". An unusually large crop of roses is sometimes taken as the sign of a harsh Winter, and if they grow profusely in Autumn an epidemic can be expected during the following year. The sinister aspects of the rose developed because the flowers were commonly used for the decoration of graves.

Snowdrop. On the one hand this delicate little flower has a divine aspect because it is supposed to resemble "an angel on a snowflake", and on the other it is a flower of doom, being associated in superstitious minds with death. However, in the garden the snowdrop is a symbol of hope and a harbinger of springtime.

Sunflower, a symbol of Christian obedience because during the day it turns its face to the sun.

Violet, the colour of penitence and mourning. In some rural areas it is considered unlucky to bring less than a handful of violets into the house. It is even more sinister if violets bloom in the Autumn when "Nature is beginning to die".

Weeds symbolize "useless abundance". They were believed by old-time peasants to grow as the outcome of the curse laid upon the land as a punishment for the sins of Adam, our first gardener. It is supposed to be impious to attempt to strip the land completely of weeds, since this is an act of rebellion against the Creator.

In cataloguing the curious superstitions associated with popular flowers we are constantly reminded that much of what is now written off as old wives' tales originally formed a comprehensive philosophy which sought to explain the purpose behind the powers of nature, a mere fragment of which now survives in the form of omens, charms and antidotes against evil. We easily recognize in flower superstitions certain features and themes which constantly recur in folklore. It is obvious that the unlucky aspect of a flower superstition almost invariably predominates, but this can perhaps be ascribed to the pessimistic outlook which influences much of our thinking.

Seeking signs and portents in nature as a guide to the future, our ancestors surveyed their environment with acute powers of observation and decided that it was an omen of misfortune if a flower blossomed out of season. Heavy-scented blooms, for example white lilac, were considered ominous because of the general belief that they housed the souls of the dead who emerged after dark to attack sleepers. Dreaming of white flowers was always a bad sign, for the simple reason that white was once the colour of mourning, as it is in the Far East today. A Western example of the same superstition is the white dove which artists use to symbolize the soul.

Flowers with yellow corollas seemed to suggest the idea of sunlight, and therefore fertility, and were correspondingly luck-bringers. Scarlet blossoms suggested the idea of blood which was once regarded as the life essence (some called it "the seat of the soul"). One of the most widely known flower superstitions relates to the bunching of red and white flowers together, which when combined become symbols of misfortune: the white representing bloodlessness and mourning; the red bloodshed. Hospital nurses will rarely if ever permit a bunch of red and white flowers to be brought into a ward as it is thought that this may be followed by the death of a patient. There is now a latter-day superstition which forbids red and white flowers being brought aboard 'planes.

The theatrical profession is notoriously superstitious and includes among its many taboos the prohibition of real flowers on the stage as being unlucky for the production and cast alike. However, since artificial flowers are considered perfectly safe, some other factor than the flowers themselves must lie behind this curious prejudice. Possibly the answer is to be found in the association of flowers with funerals and sad farewells. Saying it "with flowers" obviously has dangerous implications for those whose activities rely largely on luck for success.

It is not generally realized that fairy rings – those small circles of bright green grass which appear in the fields, usually in the older pastures – can in some circumstances be unlucky. It is especially ominous when the ring is encircled with white or yellow flowers instead of the more familiar green turf. Such places were once avoided as centres of psychically dangerous power. It was even more hazardous to sit down on the grass within the fairy ring on May Day Eve, a time when the occult forces were strongest. It was also dangerous to damage or destroy a fairy ring since this gave offence to the spirits of the field who took their revenge upon the miscreant.

Not far from Alnwick in Northumberland there used to be a fairy ring around which no child dared dance more than nine times for fear of arousing fairy anger.

Despite the aspect of gloom which surrounds so many plants it should not be forgotten that a large number of popular flowers are regarded as luck-bringers, particularly those associated in one way or another with the sun. One of these, St John's Wort (called Celestial Sun) which blooms at Midsummer, acquired its aura of sanctity because its leaves bear scarlet spots which suggested to our Christian ancestors the blood of St John the Baptist, since they usually made their appearance on the anniversary of the saint's martyrdom, June 29th. St John's Wort was placed in windows as a protection against evil spirits, phantoms, witches, storms, howling winds and lightning, hence its popular name "Devil's Flight".

> St John's Wort, scaring from the midnight heath
> The witch and goblin with its spicy breath.

It was long believed in the Isle of Man that anyone who accidentally trod on St John's Wort after sunset would be whisked away on the back of a fairy horse.

Among the less familiar superstitions are a number which indicate the close relationship between the kingdom of plants and flowers and other forms of natural life, particularly birds. Old-time farmers had a saying: "When you see the wheatear you may sow your grain", and "When the cuckoo comes to the bare thorn, then sell your cow and buy your corn." These bear testimony to a sense of the interrelationship between the creatures of Nature and the affairs of mankind.

The pleasing old-time tradition that the birds of the air were in possession of privileged information, due to their powers of flight which brought them into contact with the angel host, gave rise to the curious belief that they had an instinctive knowledge of the properties of herbs. Many of the old herbals asserted that swallows applied celandine to the eyes of baby birds to relieve dimness of sight; while eyebright was supposed to have been used for the relief of the bloodshot eyes of nestlings. Even more remarkable misinformation relating to animal life and plants was current among country folk abroad. For example, Norwegian peasants believed that the herb ossifrage reduced the bones of the animal which ate it to a kind of rubber-like substance, which rendered it incapable of standing upright. A species of sow thistle was supposed to endow the timid hare with immense courage and also provide the animal with shelter. According to Culpeper, the English herbalist, the plant moonwort has the power to pull the shoe from any horse that treads upon it, while many blacksmiths would keep a bunch of mouse-ear (to use the old name of the forget-me-not) in their forge as it would in some miraculous fashion protect the horse from injury by the blacksmith when it was shod.

Mankind derives a great deal of enjoyment from creating imaginary monsters – dragons, werewolves, vampires – which possibly explains the once widespread belief in the existence of fabulous plants. Among travellers' tales of the Middle Ages were astounding reports of trees which fathered children. An Italian named Odoricus de Foro Julii, writing in the Middle Ages, insisted that such offspring always appeared unusually radiant during a gale but had a tendency to droop on windless days.

It was also said that some trees gave birth to birds or were transformed into geese, hence the long-standing belief in the existence of a Barnacle Goose tree. As Bishop Fleetwood astutely observed in his *Curiosities of Agriculture and Gardening*, published in 1707: "A tree that bears oysters is a very extraordinary thing." He was commenting on the report of a traveller from Guadeloupe who insisted that oysters had been seen there, suspended from the branches of trees.

Another old-time writer mentioned a Chilean tree which produced worms, a serpent-bearing tree, and a molluscan plant called Catopa the leaves of which were gradually transformed into butterflies. Then there was the Wak Wak tree which grew human heads; and, perhaps oddest of all, the Vegetable Lamb Tree of Tartary which was fully described in Zahn's *Speculae Physics – Mathematics – Historical*, published in 1696: "Very wonderful is the Tartarian shrub which the natives call Boromez (i.e. lamb). It grows like a lamb to the height of about three feet." This remarkable plant was endowed with the feet, ears and hooves of a lamb, and covered by a thin bark which the natives of the locality used for the manufacture of hats. The sap of the Vegetable Lamb tree was very succulent, the pulp tasting like lobster. Yet oddly enough the only animal which really enjoyed making a meal of a Vegetable Lamb was the wolf, the other creatures of the wild shunning it like the plague.

CHAPTER FOUR

Flowers of Love

Flowers have been employed by mankind in every imaginable situation and although the superstitions with which they are associated are often of the morbid kind, there are as we have seen many extremely enjoyable aspects of flower lore. This is most obvious in traditions connected with love-making which seem to have been interwoven with floral mythology from very early times. In the realms of courtship and marriage the role of flowers has been extremely significant and is likely to continue so to judge from the siting of florists' shops near railway stations to enable the late-arriving male to purchase his peace from the wife waiting patiently at home.

Commencing with masculine floral decorations we offer several curious gems of information relating to the flower posy or buttonhole. It was not until 1879 that the word "buttonhole" entered the dictionary to describe the flower worn as a symbol of sartorial elegance. Each of the various flowers selected for this purpose has its own symbolic meaning.

The gardenia echoes the Edwardian era when flowers or nosegays appeared in the buttonhole of every fashionable man about town, an excellent choice for it is the symbol of refinement.

The red carnation, when worn as a buttonhole is not only symbolically masculine but also a symbol of love.

Any male who wears an orchid can justly claim to be an exotic.

Cornflowers were worn as buttonholes by the stage-coach drivers of nineteenth-century England. The flower symbolizes rustic life.

Finally, the posy was originally the name given to a poem which in a more romantic era accompanied the gift of a bouquet to a loved one.

Flowers have a significant role in the rituals of love and marriage. They make the ideal love gift being tokens of affection as well as subtle devices for winning the favour of the one desired. The highest mark of affection which a woman of Timor could bestow on the man she loved was to present him with a flower from her hair. To quote an old writer: "A man seeking a woman wore a white flower over his ear, and if his love grows ardent, he wears a red rose or hibiscus. But if he tires of her he puts some green thing in their place."

A floral love-signalling device is used today by English canal boat girls who intend to display their interest in a man in a passing boat who pleases them: they put a potted plant on the deck, and he knows at once that he is looked upon favourably.

Delving even more deeply into the floral lore of the past we become aware of the extent to which flowers were used as aphrodisiacs in ancient times, a fact which usually astounds those who have taken for granted the existence of a state of permanent sexual excitement among primitive lovers. Love philtres, as they were known, were designed to reanimate the sexual passions or at the very least conquer the hearts of sluggish males and females. Some of those recipes for romance were based entirely on magic.

The pansy, as we mentioned earlier, when placed over the eyes of a sleeper impelled him to make love with the first person who met his eyes on awakening. Vervain and cumin seed, especially the latter, had a "compelling power over the emotions". This charm was secretly administered by Italian peasant girls to their lovers to retain their affections. An Italian girl also wore a sprig of basil behind her ear or in her bosom when she kept an assignment. The root of the male fern and the jasmine are among other popular love flowers; the latter were woven into chaplets to the accompaniment of recited incantations.

A great deal of poetry has been dedicated to love magic and floral aphrodisiacs over the ages. To quote an old poem:

> The image of love, that nightly flies
> To visit the bashful maid,

Steals from the jasmine flower, that sighs
Its soul, like hers, in the shade.

Charles Connell, who includes a number of ready-to-hand aphrodisiacs in his amusing book, *Aphrodisiacs in Your Garden*, refers to an ancient "love tonic" prepared from ordinary garden flowers, based on the following formula: "The flowers and leaves of myrtle, two handfuls, infuse them in two quarts' spring water, and a quart of white wine, for twenty-four hours, and then distil them in a cold still, and this will be a strong scent and tincture, and by adding more or less of the myrtle, you may make it stronger or weaker as you please. This beautifies and mixed with cordial syrups is a good cordial and inclines those that drink it to be very amorous." Mr Connell does not restrict his choice of aphrodisiacs to flowers, but lays special emphasis upon the treasures of the vegetable patch. "We guarantee that he [the male] will find all the sexual boost he needs in beans, celery, lettuce, shallots, tomatoes, onions, peas, carrots, radishes, asparagus, cabbage and spinach."

Flowers are, of course, inseparable from wedding ceremonies, where they are emblems of fertility. The flower girl, who is a feature of the modern ceremony, originated from the custom of girls carrying garlands of wheat in medieval wedding processions. There was at one time a delightful tradition in which roses and rose petals were strewn in front of the bride which the seventeenth-century poet Herrick mentions in his "Hesperides":

The showers of roses, lucky foure-leav'd grasse,
The while the cloud of younglings sing
And drown ye with a flowrie spring.

Orange blossoms have served as bridal flowers for untold centuries, for they are not merely symbols of good luck and happiness but also confer fertility. There is a theory that the fashion of carrying them has a classical origin, for the orange was almost certainly the "golden apple" given to Jupiter by Juno on their wedding day. In the past the bride's head was garlanded with flowers, this being known as "the coronet of the good girl", for it was restricted to ladies of unblemished respectability.

Greek and Roman brides were crowned with marjoram, and the Roman bridegroom decked himself with myrtle on his wedding day. In Indian weddings a wreath of flowers provided the bond which united the bridal pair. There was a custom at Oldenburg in Germany in which the bridegroom had his bed linen especially embroidered with flower motifs combined with a tree, a cock bird, and his initials.

One of the prettiest of the social rites designed to bring luck in marriage involves the throwing of the bouquet by the bride to her bridesmaids following the ceremony. According to an old belief the bridesmaid who catches the flowers is destined to be the next to marry.

The poet Quarles describes in his "Sheapheard's Oracles" which he wrote in 1646 how:

> Love sick swains
> Comprise rush-rings and myrtle-berry chains.
> And stuck with glorious kingcups and their bonnets
> Adorn'd with laurell slips, chaunt their love sonnets.

which brings us to the pleasing subject of the language of love.

In Folkard's monumental work, *Plant Lore, Legends and Lyrics,* the author introduces the mysterious subject of flower language thus: "The antiquity of floral emblems probably dates from the time when the human heart first beat with the gentle emotions of affection or throbbed with the wild pulsations of love." Early man apparently acquired this understanding from the study of flowers: "In the struggle to learn the properties of plants in order to obtain wholesome food man found that with the beauty of their form and colour they spoke lovingly to him."

Whatever might have been the source of the art of communication between human beings, it must be assumed that the invention of floral languages in the form of symbols was the product of sophisticated society rather than that of the so-called barbarian races.

Anglo-Saxon England had little room for the softer metaphors of affection, being concerned largely with the masculine aggressive aspect of human relationships, and in this emotionally arid climate floral art tended to wilt.

Flower and plant symbols have been found decorating the ruined palaces of ancient civilizations, and even caves and rock temples, where men and women of forgotten cults honoured strange gods. There are references in the literature of the East to

Flowers of Love

the use of flowers as tokens of communication, as for example when a slave begged liberty from his master in ancient Persia, saying, "Do good to thy servant whilst thou hast the power, for the season of power is often as transient as the duration of this beautiful flower." At the same time he would hand him a rose – a gesture which earned him immediate liberty.

We find in the books of ancient India flower symbols in abundance, but even more so among the Greeks who elevated the art to a sophisticated cult which flourished until the decline of Greece as a force in human culture.

There are many groupings of flower symbols, but the ones that concern us most are associated with the love between men and women. In medieval Europe special values were accorded to colours in dress and ornament. This system included the wearing of flowers of particular colours to indicate one's feelings at a given time. The romances of the age of chivalry echo this principle most eloquently. In *The Romance of Perceforet*, the gift of a hat adorned with roses embodies a message of love to its recipient. Closer to our own time is the age of Shakespeare with its frequent references to flower language, as in the description of Ophelia: ". . . with fantastic garlands did she come, Of crow-flowers, nettles, daisies, and long purples . . ." whose combined message reads: "A fair maid stung to the quick; her virgin bloom under the cold hand of death."

The language of flowers was one of the secret arts evolved in the harems of Turkey for illicit communication between lovers, and also as a means of idling away the time. This curious code was introduced into England by Lady Wortley Montague, the eighteenth-century English poetess and letter-writer who travelled extensively in Asia where she discovered many of the secrets of the harem. The language was also known in France, having been introduced there by La Mortrae who shared the exile of Charles XII of Sweden.

There has existed more than one language of flowers, each of them a worthy memorial to the lost art of floral communication, which in its heyday must have made the love affair a very delicate experience indeed. The development of flower language to a fine art must be credited to the Victorians who arranged their posies in special ways in order to establish explicit messages. In this fashion a bunch of flowers could be made to "speak volumes", demanding in response a mere flutter of eyelashes or a subtle movement of a fan. Students of Victorian manners have described the incongruity in the relationship between the sexes which sanctioned the utmost extremes of licence provided that the object of the passion belonged to the poorer classes or that the affair was conducted in secret. At the same time the custodians of morality insisted upon an official code of courtship which was almost oriental in its contrived reticence.

The laws of courtship differ from age to age, but all have as their common factor the implicit rule that the first approach must be made by the male, although in practice it is the female who signals her interest. To an extent the language of love by-passed this barrier providing an easily interpreted style of communication which could be conducted at two levels: as a light-hearted flirtation or as the prelude to a serious assignment.

As an example of the language of love in action let us consider an imaginary situation in which the passionate Mr Jones wishes to convey his amorous sentiments to the coy but obviously interested Miss Smith. For the purpose of this exercise we have also to imagine that all the flowers required for this "conversation" are in bloom at the same time. Mr Jones advances, wearing in his buttonhole a daffodil which symbolizes "regard". Miss Smith responds by arranging the flowers in the drawing-room vase with a finger tenderly caressing a Canterbury bell, representing "acknowledgement". The message received, Mr Jones signals his further intentions by means of hawthorn blossom indicating "hope", to which he is given the flower thrift, meaning "sympathy". The charade can continue on the same lines almost indefinitely:

Mr Jones, now inflamed, sets his amorous eyes on Miss Smith and offers her a dwarf sunflower: "adoration". Miss Smith responds with a morning glory: "affection". Mr Jones offers a rose: "love". Miss Smith warns against impetuosity with a rhododendron: "danger". Mr Jones (forcefully) desires return of affection, the token of which is a jonquil. Miss Smith submits – red tulip: "I love".

How one conveyed one's affections during seasons when the particular flower representing one's sentiments happened to be out of bloom remains a mystery which only gardeners or lovers can reveal.

A complete alphabet of love flowers follows. It incorporates the ancient and modern love symbolism in order to provide a truly comprehensive vocabulary for those who wish to restore to flowers their traditional role in the art of courtship.

Code d'Amour – The Language of Love

Flower or Plant	*Ancient Meaning*	*Modern Meaning*
Acacia	Pure love	Friendship
Acanthus	Love of the arts	The arts
Agrimony	–	Thankfulness
Almond	–	Indiscretion
Aloe	–	Grief
Amaranth	Fidelity	Immortality
Amaryllis	–	Pride
Anemone	Abandonment	Forsaken
Angelica	Gentle sorrow	Inspiration
Apple blossom	–	Preference
Asphodel	–	Regrets
Aster – China	Elegance	Variety
Balsam	Impatience	Impatience
Barberry	–	Sour disposition
Basil	Poverty	Hatred
Borage	–	Bluntness
Broom	–	Humility
Buttercup	Sarcasm	Ingratitude
Canterbury bell	Acknowledgement	Constancy
Carnation	–	Alas my poor heart
Cinquefoil	Mother love	My beloved daughter
Clematis	–	Deceit
Columbine	–	Folly
Convolvulus	–	Night
Coriander	–	Concealed worth
Cowslip	–	I worship you
Daffodil	Regard	Self-love
Dahlia	–	Instability
Daisy	–	Innocence
Dandelion	Oracle	Rural oracle
Dittany	Discretion	Childbirth
Eglantine	–	Poetry

Flower or Plant	*Ancient Meaning*	*Modern Meaning*
Fleur-de-luce	–	Flame
Forget-me-not	Remembrance and faith	Forget me not
Foxglove	–	Insincerity
Geranium	Folly	Deception
Hawthorn	–	Hope
Heart's-ease	–	Think of me
Heath	–	Solitude
Hollyhock	–	Ambition
Honeysuckle	We are united in love	Generous love
Hop	–	Injustice
Hyacinth	Amenity	Play
Ice plant	–	You freeze me
Iris	I am indifferent	Message
Ivy	I am attached to you	Friendship
Jasmine	Amiability	Good nature
Jonquil	Amorous languor	I desire you
Juniper	–	Protection
Lavender	Silence	Mistrust
Leaves – dead	–	Melancholy
Lilac	Love stirs in me	Love stirs in me
Lilac – white	–	Youth
Lily	Purity and majesty	Majesty
Lily of the Valley	–	Return of happiness
London Pride	–	Frivolity
Lotus	–	Eloquence
Maple	–	Reserve
Marigold	–	Grief
Marvel of Peru	Flame of love	Timidity
Meadow Saffron	–	My best days have passed
Mignonette	–	Your qualities surpass your charms
Moonwort	Bad payment	Forgetfulness
Morning Glory	–	Affection
Moss	–	Maternal love
Musk plant	–	Weakness
Myrtle	Love	Love
Narcissus	Foolish self-esteem	Self-love

Flower or Plant	*Ancient Meaning*	*Modern Meaning*
Orange flower	Virginity	Chastity
Pansy	–	Thoughts
Passion flower	–	Faith
Peony	Shame	Shame/bashfulness
Periwinkle	Unbreakable friendship	Tender memories
Pink	Pure love	Pure love
Poppy	Sleep	Consolation/sleep
Primrose	–	Childhood
Rhododendron	–	Danger
Rose	Love and beauty	Love
Rose – musk	–	Capricious beauty
Rose – single	–	Simplicity
Rose – white	–	Silence
Rose – withered	–	Declining beauty
Rose – yellow	–	Unfaithful
Rosebud	–	Girlhood
Rosemary	Revival of vitality	I am revitalized by you
Saffron	–	Beware of excess
St John's Wort	–	Superstition
Snapdragon	–	You are presumptuous
Snowdrop	–	Hope
Speedwell	–	Fidelity
Star of Bethlehem	–	Purity
Stock	–	Lasting beauty
Sunflower	Adoration	False riches
Sweet-william	–	Happiness
Thrift	–	Sympathy
Thyme	Spontaneous emotion	Activity
Tuberose	–	Dangerous pleasures
Tulip	Grandeur	A declaration of love
Venus' Looking-glass	–	Flattery
Vervain	Pure affection	Enchantment
Violet	Modesty	Modesty
Violet – white	–	Innocence
Wallflower	–	Fidelity in misfortune

The language of flowers was never more beautifully expressed than in the Valentine cards fashionable during the Victorian era, a further indication of the desire for amorous and secret forms of communication among our great-grandparents. At the centre of each beautifully engraved card would be depicted a posy of flowers indicating the secret message intended for the recipient. Apart from the romantic impact of a missive from out of the blue so to speak, it reaffirmed the old tradition that a posy could speak volumes in a delicate situation which precluded an open expression of feeling.

Flower superstition, symbolism and love magic lay at the root of a custom in which a woman would insert a sprig of myrtle between the pages of a prayer book containing the marriage service. The myrtle was then placed under the lady's pillow overnight, and if it had mysteriously vanished by the morning it was a happy omen for the future.

As a variation upon the various languages of love we find that a curious system of floral divination was practised by girls when they desired to ascertain the true character of the one they loved. In essence, this was no more than a lottery – a game of chance in which vital decisions were submitted to the arbitration of the spirits. Numbers were written on pieces of paper, each representing a particular flower and were then placed in a box from which they were afterwards drawn in the manner of the lucky dip. These numbers were checked with the following table. Any suitor who received a "certificate of unworthiness" was rejected.

Number	*Flower*	*Characteristic*
1	Ranunculus	Enterprising
2	Wild Pink	Foolish
3	Auricula	Base
4	Blue Cornflower	Talkative
5	Wild Orach	Indolent
6	Daisy	Gentle
7	Tulip	Showy
8	Jonquil	Obstinate
9	Orange flower	Over-hasty
10	Rose	Over-submissive
11	Amaranth	Arbitrary

Number	*Flower*	*Characteristic*
12	Stock	Greedy
13	Arum	Ardour
14	Asphodel	Languishing
15	Tricolorus	Very selfish
16	Tuberose	Ambitious
17	Jasmine	Cheerful
18	Heart's-ease	Delicate
19	Lily	Sincere
20	Fritillary	A coquette
21	Snapdragon	Presumptuous
22	Carnation	Capricious
23	Marigold	Jealous type
24	Everlasting flower	Honest and reliable

Continuing on the theme of love and affection, brief reference must be made to several plants which were specifically designated "love plants". Among these we find love-lies-bleeding which derived its name from the fanciful connection between the crimson flowers and an effusion of blood; and the *Clematis vitalba* or traveller's joy which was once called "Love" because its habit of climbing was comparable with the human sexual embrace. There were also love-in-a-chain, love-in-idleness otherwise the pansy, and loveman.

Looking through old books on the folklore of flowers and plants it is interesting to discover how so many of the plants which had originally been dedicated to Venus were later, in Christian times, reallocated to the Virgin Mary. However, a few continue to be linked by name with the pagan goddess of love, among them such exotics as Venus' basin (the teasel), Venus' chariot drawn by doves (monkshood), Venus-in-her-car (water betony) and Venus' looking-glass (the corn bellflower).

To move from the flowers of love to those associated with death is but a mournful stroll from Midsummer's joy to Winter's darkness, a time when all that is verdant (save the evergreen) withers in the fields and finally dies. In the very earliest writings we find solemn allusions to the link between death's grim reaper and the plant world, as when trees were planted on tombs in classical times to serve as symbols or even embodiments of the souls of the departed. The ancient dead were almost invariably buried amid groves of sacred trees, for we learn from Grotius that among the Greeks and Romans there existed the belief that souls delighted to stroll in these arboreal "temples". The Greeks strewed the graves of those they loved with myrtle, polyanthus and aramanthe. For those who died young there were spring and summer flowers, while the old were commemorated by ancient trees and aromatic herbs.

There was once a callous practice among the Welsh of "casting scorn" upon the graves of old bachelors and old maids by planting their graves with nettles, thistles, henbane and other noxious weeds, a reference perhaps to the dislike once felt for infertility. On the other hand, when a young unmarried person died the grave would be strewn with evergreens and flowers since the dead were "laying in their nuptial beds and not in their graves". White roses were planted on the tombs of virgins, and red ones where the deceased had lived an exemplary life. Only sweet-scented flowers were used especially rosemary, hyssop, sweet-williams, gillyflowers and carnations. At a virgin's funeral it was long the custom for a young girl to lead the procession wearing a garland of flowers which was later hung above the pew in the church where the dead girl had worshipped. These "maids' gardens", faded and dusty, can still be seen in old churches – their meaning forgotten, but often preserved because of the superstition that it is unlucky to remove them.

Even cremation in ancient times involved the burning of branches of yew, cypress and fir on the funeral pyres which sent heavenward an aromatic scent. In old England rosemary was borne by mourners to the graveside and thrown upon the coffin before it was lost to sight.

> To show their love, the neighbours far and near
> Followed with wistful looks and damsel's bier.
> Sprigged Rosemary, the lads and lasses bore,
> While dismally the parson walked before.
>
> John Gay, from his series of pastorals

In the byways of folklore we still find a number of curious funeral customs involving flowers. A curious roadside ritual is carried out by persons unknown (possibly gypsies) on the highway about three and a half miles from Newmarket in Suffolk. Flowers are regularly laid on the grave of a shepherd boy who committed suicide about two hundred years ago and was

Flowers of the Silence

buried, as was then the custom, at the cross-roads. It is considered unlucky for travellers not to place a flower or at least a coin on the grave when passing the spot. In Devonshire there is a similar roadside grave, that of a girl suicide named Jane or Jay which is always bedecked with flowers left there, some say, by the pixies.

Even in that melancholy ante-chamber of life, the Realm of the Dead, sweet-scented flowers were given an important role. There is a belief among Spiritualists that flowers grow in profusion in "Summerland", the spiritualist "Heaven". The blossoms being spiritual in essence are impervious to the destructive workings of time.

The modern funeral ceremony has by no means displaced the use of flowers at burials, although flower-lovers often insert a clause in their wills: No Flowers By Request. Today's mourners favour winter-flowering heather, aubrietia, the miniature rose and the traditional rosemary for this solemn occasion.

CHAPTER FIVE

Healing Flowers

During the past few centuries the physician has replaced the priest as the mystical master of ceremonies who supervises the welfare of mankind, for who will deny that health is the preoccupation of all? Vast fortunes are expended on medications, whole armies of chemists are employed in the production of drugs to ensure that we shall be relieved of pain and discomfort and that our days shall be long.

Much of this wealth of medical resources is comparatively new to mankind. For untold centuries medicine as we know it today was undreamed of, and for the maintenance of good health our ancestors relied upon the plants of the hedgerows and the herbs of the field. Vegetables and flowers played a vital role in early medicine, and were chosen empirically, that is, on the basis of their proven worth, or according to a curious medical system known as the Doctrine of Signatures.

This system involved judging the medical potentialities of a plant from its outward appearance, or from some real or fancied resemblance to the particular part of the human anatomy it was intended to treat. By modern standards its underlying principles might seem insane. Because garlic had a ruddy hue it was used as a medicine for blood disorders, and was supposed in addition to relieve ailments of the windpipe because it had a hollow stalk.

Not only wild plants, but vegetables and garden flowers were utilized by healers who had mastered the art of interpreting the clues or "signatures" displayed upon stalks, leaves and petals. For example, the lungwort or *Pulmonaria*, which bore markings not dissimilar to tubercular scars, was prescribed for consumption, while the Canterbury bell or throatwort with its throat-like corolla was an obvious specific for bronchitis. Other herbs and plants indicated by their names their particular medical function, e.g. nipple wort, spleen wort and kidney vetch.

It is also evident that the "signature", by means of which the healing property of a plant might be recognized, was by no means limited to outward signs but included its specific functions, an example being the *Saxifraga,* known as breakstones from its habit of splitting rocks as the result of the seeds taking root in the cracks. In consequence it was used for the treatment of calculi, the solid concretions which occur in the bodily organs. In the main, however, it was some imagined resemblance to a medical condition which determined the choice of a particular herb or plant as a healing agent.

Briony has imprinted on its root a mark which is similar to the feet of a dropsical person, and was therefore recommended as a cure for dropsy. *Prunella* or *Brunella,* also known as brownwort because of its brownish leaves, was used to treat a kind of quinsy; and because the corolla of this particular plant had a profile which looked not unlike a billhook it was given the local name carpenter's herb and used for the treatment of wounds caused by sharp-edged tools.

Our ancestors firmly believed in the ancient doctrine of the Four Humours and this had a profound influence upon the development of herbal medicines. The Four Humours divided all healing knowledge and practice into four watertight compartments, based upon the principles of dryness, moisture, heat and cold respectively, each of which embraced a specific bodily condition: blood, phlegm, black bile, and yellow bile. Yellow-hued plants were supposed to increase yellow bile and brownish, spotted and blackish plants were used for the treatment of black bile. White flowers with a viscous sap suggested the idea of phlegm and were employed for its cure, while red-coloured flowers were expected to purify the blood, and so on. Milky plants were thought to increase the flow of mammary milk. Those plants and flowers which happened to combine several qualities were used to treat more than one ailment.

The reasoning of our ancestors as it was applied to the healing arts had as its outcome a number of very curious medical theories. For example, lettuce, willow and fern were thought to cause male sterility, while "salacious and fecund plants" were expected to confer fertility.

It has been suggested that the real importance of the Doctrine of Signatures was that despite its deficiencies it laid the basis for the systematic study of botany. For just as alchemy had fathered scientific chemistry and astrology had evolved into astronomy, so the Doctrine of Signatures developed by our ancestors in their quest for relief from sickness paved the way for the scientific study of plants, flowers and trees.

It was in fact no less a naturalist than John Ray who expressed the view that although the Doctrine of Signatures might be unreliable, there was at least an element of reasoning behind the system, and possibly a basis of truth, for he wrote: "Howbeit, I will not deny that, but that the noxious and malignant plants do many of them discover something of their nature by the sad and melancholick visage of their leaves flowers or fruits."

Nevertheless, it becomes obvious when studying ancient books of herbal lore how extravagant were the aspirations of the old herbalists. Indeed, ailments which even now lie well beyond the range of scientific medicine were confidently claimed as curable by the advocates of the Doctrine of Signatures. Not only were malignant diseases supposed to be repelled by the relevant herb or plant but, strange to say, also vipers, dragons, monsters and similar demonic creatures. That famous work, *Plant Lore, Legend and Lyrics,* describes how herbalists "could prevent the hair falling out and also restore it to the bald pate, and could turn it yellow, red or black by their mystical arts. They cured lunacy, relieved anxiety and purged melancholy: to say nothing of counteracting witchcraft and the malignant influence of the mysterious evil eye" – by magical herbs.

Each part of the human anatomy was associated with its curative plant, and these were tabulated in the old herbals for easy reference:

Bladder: bladderwort, nasturtium, senna leaves, black hellebore
Ears: mountain bindweed, gentian, hypericum
Eyes: acacia, daisy, hyacinth, geranium, narcissus, cornflower
Fingers, hands and the nervous system: garlic, shepherd's purse, geranium, satyrion, plantain, currants, swallow wort

Hair: goat's beard, fennel, vine and vine roots etc.
Head: antirrhinum, crocus, geranium, walnuts
Heart: borage, motherwort, strawberries, pomegranate blossom, violet, peony, rose, iris, lotus
Intestines: navel wort, briony, dodder, honeysuckle, nasturtium
Kidneys: kidney wort, broom seeds, jasmine, lupin seeds, ground ivy
Liver: noble liverwort, aloe, Our Lady's thistle, lettuce
Lungs: lungwort, garden teasel, cresses, rhubarb, valerian
Spleen: spleenwort, shepherd's purse, dandelion, fern, broom, hawkweed
Stomach: cyclamen, elecampane, iris, parsnip, radish, chives
Teeth: fir and juniper leaves, sunflower seed, toothed violet, dandelion
Tongue: adder tongue, hound's tongue, sunflower seed

The older generation of herbal healers regarded a mystical incantation as a vitally necessary supplement to the treatment of the sick and they prescribed Judas Ear, a woodland fungus which seems to have had quasi-miraculous qualities, in conjunction with the following oral charm:

For the cough take Judas Eare,
With the parynge of a Peare.
And drynke them without fear
If you will have remedy.
The syppes are for the hyckocke
And six more for the chyckocke
Thus my pretty pyckocke
Recover by and by.

For the treatment of fever one scratched a Latin charm with a pin on a laurel leaf which was laid beneath the sufferer's pillow and he was then left to the care of nature and the Lord.

Most of the old botanical charms have been forgotten, although Charles Bowness declares in his book *Romany Magic* that gypsies still resort to incantations when treating their sick.

Pain my head
Go to the Devil, your father
You have hurt my head
Now go away from me

Home to the Devil.
Go to the Evil One.
Whoever treads on my shadow
Let him have the pain.

And again when bathing sore eyes:

Pain from my eyes, go into the water
Go into the saffron, go into the earth
Go to the earth devil
That is your home.

A gypsy protects himself against rheumatic pains by carrying several horse-chestnuts in his pocket. The blue flower of the speedwell, boiled in rainwater, provided it is collected on the first of May, makes an ideal eye wash and also a drink to relieve the cataract. Yet another well-known gypsy treatment for arthritis is the water in which stinging nettles have been boiled.

Turning for the moment to the baneful aspects of plant lore one thinks automatically of the lethal belladonna which was once extensively used by Italian poisoners. This is a plant of ill-omen, the favourite of witches. Then we have the mandrake, a plant of mystery which is considered by many to have been the earliest known anaesthetic, for under its old name the "Death Wine" it was given to those condemned to suffer on the cross in ancient Rome, with the aim of shortening their agonies by stupefaction. Henbane, yet another of the ancient lethal herbs, became the source of the drug "twilight sleep". Among similar plants which have been incorporated into modern medicine are the poppy, monkshood and wild hemlock with which the philosopher Socrates took his life in 399 B.C. Hemlock, like belladonna, was taken as a narcotic by those condemned to painful execution.

There is a strongly established rural superstition that a poisonous plant and its antidote invariably grow together, a popular example being the stinging nettle and dock which are found close to one another; also that as both rheumatism and the willow "occur" in damp areas they are therefore related, one of the old cures for rheumatism being an extract of willow.

It has to be made clear to readers that any amateur investigation of the curative properties of plants and flowers must be avoided at all cost, for many are extremely dangerous. Broom causes stomach burn and paralysis, dog's mercury serious

Dreamless Sleep

stomach upsets, the lesser celandine and buttercup cause dermatitis, lily of the valley affects the heart, cuckoo pint can kill and the common rhododendron affects the health of livestock.

The closer the subject is studied, the more it becomes apparent that a primary reason why herbal lore was considered effective in ancient times was the magical aura which surrounded it. As Brian Inglis says in his book *Fringe Medicine*: "In a community impressed by magic, the effect of treatment with herbs could be powerfully reinforced with the suggestion that they had special properties because they had been picked on a blasted heath by the seventh son of a seventh son, or by a one-eyed crone at full moon." This mystical approach he suggested had a tendency to undermine respect for the genuine healing properties of a particular herb, plant or flower.

Today's herbalism has apparently shed its mysticism and is firmly based on "scientific" principles. One wonders, however, whether the new herbalism is quite as effective as the magical plant lore of yesterday's rural "pharmacists" with their mind-bending magical litanies and supernatural brews.

Among the disregarded treasures of rural households there are curious manuscript books, often re-written from even older books, containing skin remedies and recipes for cosmetics belonging to great-great-grandmother's day. Our forefathers and their spouses drew extensively upon the countryside for the ingredients, their cures often proving far more effective than the products now readily obtainable from the chemist's shop. Elderflower water provided a skin tonic suitable for sensitive skins, and the flower itself made a useful hand-salve. A compress of hollyhock leaves when liquefied soothed sunburned or roughened skins; similarly, buttercup ointment was helpful for the treatment of sore hands.

Daphne Barraclough, in her *Flower-Lover's Miscellany*, refers to a sixteenth-century recipe for "complexion water" based on lavender flowers: "Take a gallon of faire water, one handfull of lauender flowres and some few cloues and orace powder and foure ounces of Benjamin [a vegetable gum], distill the water in an ordinarie leaden still."

A cowslip bath could be prepared from three handfuls of cowslip flowers which had to be put into a bag and immersed in hot water. Such a bath was guaranteed to relax the entire body and induce a sense of complete tranquillity.

An old Worcestershire recipe for hair tonic contained four parts' fresh herbs to one of dried: rosemary 2oz., southernwood 2oz., camphor ½oz. These were steeped in boiling water and left for an hour. The mixture was then strained and applied to the scalp twice daily.

In that happily almost forgotten era of chilblains one resorted to "a poultice of boiled turnips and afterwards another of boiled groundsel" for a cure. In an extreme case one could always thrash the chilblains with holly, keeping the legs tightly crossed when doing so. Should this fail, you might adopt an old-time Cornish healing ritual which entails standing on one's head for a quarter of an hour.

CHAPTER SIX

Flower Myths and Legends

A strange area of human experience is opened up when one peers into the past to rediscover the lost legends of the human race. This is particularly the case with the traditions surrounding flowers which under investigation prove to be something more than fairy tale and classical legend, and closer to the imaginative world of the child of our own day. There is a kind of primitive innocence in those doleful sagas in which a delicate maiden obtains refuge from the undesired caresses of a rampant male by assuming, with the consent of the appropriate deity, the shape of a plant which is especially created for the occasion. After concentrating upon the sad fates of so many hapless maids in the past it becomes almost impossible to look at one's garden in a rational way.

Or could it be said that only after one has absorbed the strange lore of the flower world does one begin to understand flowers at all.

Acacia. The acacia was the source of the wood used in building the Ark of the Covenant and from this tree came the thorns with which Christ was crowned before His crucifixion. An ancient Egyptian legend tells how a human soul was once concealed in the topmost branches of the acacia tree, but when the tree was cut down its owner passed away. Only after an acacia seed pod had been placed in water and given to the corpse, did the dead man revive, becoming in time the Pharaoh of Egypt. A sprig of the acacia is one of the symbolic flowers of Freemasonry.

Almond. The ancient world displayed a great deal of interest in this beautiful plant, which was associated with the legend of the youth Demophoon, who after falling deeply in love with the Princess Phyllis abandoned her for another. On learning of her betrayal the wretched Phyllis died of a broken heart, but was mercifully transformed by the gods into an almond tree. When he heard of her fate, Demophoon became overwhelmed with grief and, clasping his arms around the trunk of the almond tree, he burst into tears, whereupon it began to bloom out of sheer happiness. And this is the reason why the Greeks gave the beautiful name Phyllia to the almond tree.

In another medieval legend a young monk received instructions to water a small almond tree daily for two years, a task which involved conveying water from the River Nile some two miles away across the desert. After many such weary journeys the monk's efforts were rewarded when a dried branch of the tree suddenly burst into flower before his eyes.

Amaranth. This "never-fading flower" was supposed to cover the fields of Paradise, for it was one of the symbols of immortality in Greek mythology. In Roman Catholic lands churches are decorated with amaranths on Ascension Day because of their association with the after-life. Among the older names enjoyed by the amaranth are flower gentle, flower velure and velvet flower. It is believed by Swiss peasants that anyone desiring invisibility should wear an amaranth on Ascension Day.

Anemone. This is a flower of sorrow and death for it is the metamorphosis of Adonis, the favourite of Venus, who was killed by a wild boar. Anemones were placed by the Romans upon the altar of Venus, and they also provided a medicine for the treatment of malarial fevers. The Germans knew the anemone as "the little wind rose", regarding it as the metamorphosis of Chloris, a nymph of ancient legend. It is a curious fact that the Chinese, like the Greeks, associate this flower with grief.

Arum. The ancient Germans believed that where the arum prospered the wood spirits were happiest. It was also said that when Aaron's rod was planted in the ground the first Arum sprouted from the soil as a symbol of abundance. The plant has a strange sexual symbolism, for in many parts of the world superstitious farmers assess the fertility of the forthcoming year from the size of the Arum's spadix. Should it be large they rejoice; if otherwise they prepare to mourn. The Arum lies under the domination of Mars.

Broom. This is the *planta genista,* which gave its name to the Plantagenet line of English monarchs after Geoffrey, Count of Anjou, had worn it as an emblem in his helmet as he led his troops into battle in 1140. On plucking the broom from the earth Geoffrey had cried to his followers: "This golden plant shall be my cognizance, rooted firmly among rocks, yet upholding what is ready to fall. I will maintain it on the field, in the tourney, and in the court of justice." He afterwards adopted the name *planta genista,* transmitting it to his descendants. A curious Christian legend tells us how the rustling and cracking of the broom almost betrayed the whereabouts of Mary and the infant Jesus to Herod's murderous soldiers. It was the broom upon which witches of old were supposed to ride through the skies at night. There is a curious domestic superstition associated with the plant: "Sweep the house with blossomed broom in May/You are sure to sweep the head of the house away."

The *Camellia* derived its name from Kamel, a Moravian Jesuit who discovered it in the Philippines and presented it to Maria Theresa, Queen of Spain in 1639. Before Dumas the younger endowed it with its present sinister symbolism in his *Lady of the Camellias,* the white flower was a recognized emblem of purity.

Carnation. There has been a great deal of debate as to the source of the name, some relating it to *carne,* or flesh, and others to coronation because the flower had adorned ancient garlands and crowns. Because of an ancient tragedy the Italian family of Ronsecco incorporated a carnation in its coat of arms. The flower had been the farewell gift from the Countess Margharita Ronsecco to her newly-wedded husband Orlando before he embarked to fight the Saracens in the Holy Land. On hearing of his death the countess planted carnation seeds in his memory. When the first plant budded it displayed a white flower with a heart of red, a phenomenon never previously observed.

Chrysanthemum. This flower, which has been called "The Queen of the Autumn", is the product of the artistry of the florists of China and Japan. There is a curious Chinese legend dating to the third century B.C. which tells how a king of China seeking anxiously for an elixir of eternal life, discovered that the secret lay in a plant which could only be picked by the pure of heart. Three hundred virgin youths and girls were promptly dispatched to search for it. Needless to say they never returned having, presumably, lost their collective virginity *en route*. Chrysanthemums are found everywhere in Japan apart from Himeji, where they are considered unlucky for the following reason. Many years ago a girl named Okiku (kiku means chrysanthemum) was employed by a powerful nobleman to look after his works of art, which included brasses, porcelain, carvings and jewels, and ten beautiful dishes of gold. One morning Okiku discovered that a gold dish was missing, and fearing punishment she threw herself into a well where her corpse was later discovered. Ever afterwards Okiku's ghost has returned at night to count the golden dishes, one by one. When nine have been counted she fills the air with lamentations. From the time of her suicide the kiku, or chrysanthemum, has never been grown in Himeji where it is regarded as a fatal flower.

Clover. The red and white clovers which grow so freely in our meadows are one of the chief sources of pollen for the bees. Consequently clover has long been the symbol of good luck, and even more so if it has four leaves. We use the old phrase "living in clover" to denote a life of luxury, while to dream of clover is a message from fate that good fortune and health will be ours. Clover has long been regarded as a charm against evil spirits, and farmers believed that a handful picked from a neighbour's field made their own cattle healthy. In a love litany associated with the clover we are told:

> A clover, a clover of two
> Put it in your right shoe.
> The first young man you meet
> In field street or lane
> You'll have him or one of his name.

The name Clover is derived from a Latin word meaning club, the three leaflets of the clover having been likened to the triple-headed club borne by the Greek hero Hercules. Another old legend of French origin accounts for the presence of red clover at St Noch, New Orleans. A bride died on the eve of her marriage, and her distraught lover committed suicide by her tomb, his blood flowing over the soil. Ever afterwards, clover growing on this site bore a scarlet spot upon the leaves in memory of the tragedy of the two lovers.

Columbine, the English name for the Aquilegia, is derived from *colomba*, the Latin word for dove. This is perhaps due to "the resemblance of its nectaries to the heads of pigeons around a dish, a favourite device of ancient artists . . ." to quote Folkard's *Plant Lore, Legends and Lyrics*, and for a similar reason it was also known as dove wort. The columbine has played an important role in the symbolism of heraldry: combined with the red rose it forms the badge of the Royal House of Lancaster. The flower is also associated with the old-time pantomime in which the lovers, Harlequin and Columbine, were transformed into creatures of wonder. In former times this flower, like the willow, was a well-known symbol of infidelity, as we see from the couplet by Sir Thomas Browne:

> The columbine by lonely wanderer taken
> Is there ascribed to such who are forsaken.

Cowslip. According to the seventeenth-century astrologer/herbalist, Nicholas Culpeper, the Greeks gave the name "Paralysis" to this flower because they believed it to be both a remedy for palsy and beneficial to the nerves and brain. The drooping blooms suspended from each of the stalks resemble a bunch of keys, and consequently the flower acquired the names Our Lady's keys, the keys of heaven, St Peter's keys, and herb Peter. In Lancashire and parts of Kent the cowslip is called the fairies' cup because the "little people" are supposed to nestle in its blooms.

Crocus. This is one of the many flowers which symbolizes the metamorphosis of man into plant. A beautiful youth named Crocus fell deeply in love with a shepherdess named Smilax, who did not return his love. To ease his pain he was transformed by the gods into the flower which bears his name, while Smilax was changed into a yew tree. For this reason garlands of crocuses were borne by the Greeks at their marriage feasts. In ancient times the crocus was dedicated to Helios the sun god, and in the Middle Ages it became the flower of St Valentine since it was expected to bloom at dawn on St Valentine's Day.

Dahlia. This beautiful plant, a native of Mexico, was first mentioned in 1651. It bloomed with such splendour when planted at Malmaison that the Empress Josephine declared it her favourite flower and permitted neither bloom, seed nor root to be taken from her gardens. Her possessiveness tempted a Polish prince who had fallen in love with the flower, to bribe one of the gardeners to steal a hundred plants for which he paid a louis apiece. On discovering her loss the outraged Josephine refused to grow the dahlia again. The flower was introduced into England on two separate occasions, each of which coincided with some upheaval in the political life of Europe. The first occurred in 1789 at the time of the outbreak of the French Revolution, and the second when Napoleon was crowned Emperor of France. It was for these reasons that the dahlia became the recognized symbol of instability.

Daisy. The legend associated with the daisy or *Bellis* relates how Belles, a forest nymph, was pursued by lecherous Vertumnus, the deity who guarded orchards. Just in time Belles was transformed into the humble flower we call the daisy. According to the poet Chaucer, Queen Alceste was also changed into a daisy, doubtless because she possessed as many virtues as the daisy bore florets: "The great goodness of the Queen Alceste/ That was turned into a daisie." The ancient English name for the flower was Day's Eye because it closes its petals at dusk and reopens them at dawn. According to an old and somewhat sombre superstition it is necessary to place your foot on the first daisy you see in spring, otherwise the daisies will cover you before the year is out, hence no doubt the old saying "kicking up daisies" as an euphemism for death.

Dandelion. In a strange old legend we are told how the dandelions first made their appearance in the world. In ancient times when the earth was populated by elemental spirits – fairies, gnomes and elves, garbed in bright coloured gowns – the feet of the first man began to wreak havoc in the fairy kingdom. The gnomes immediately took refuge beneath the earth, the elves concealed themselves among the rocks, the brownies fled in terror to the shelter of hollow trees, while the sun-loving fairies having no hiding place were transformed into plants. A number of fairies wearing yellow garments who stood staring sadly at the sun were finally metamorphosed into dandelions. Dandelions seem to have an almost supernatural capacity for survival. Uproot them from the lawn, saturate them with weed-killers: within a week or two their yellow heads will reassert their presence in the grass. Invincibility is reaffirmed by the manner of their seeding – the small feathery seeds being blown in the wind until they come to rest and tenaciously and irremovably take root.

The name dandelion is a corruption of the French *dent de lion* meaning lion's tooth which the petals are thought to resemble. An Alonquin legend tells us how the south wind fell in love with a beautiful slender girl with sun-burnished yellow hair who was transformed into the golden flower of the American fields and meadows. In Scotland the dandelion, like many other yellow flowers, is called Gowan, which means gold.

The dandelion is another plant that plays a useful part in rustic time-keeping by indicating the hour when no other clock is available, the petals opening and closing according to the length of the day.

> Thus in each flower and simple bell
> That in our path betrodden be
> Are sweet remembrancers who tell
> How fast their winged moments fly.

Edelweiss. The edelweiss which grows on the Alpine snowline, is familiar to most English readers as "a flower of the mountain heights". According to legend Edelweiss was originally an angel who, wearying of the delights of Paradise, decided to visit the realm of earth. However, being a sensitive creature she chose to live afar from gross humanity with all its cruelties and discontents and made her home on a mountain-top where she could belong to the world and yet remain apart from it. Alas, she attracted the attentions of lustful men and in despair asked to be taken back into Heaven, leaving the flower edelweiss as a symbol of her temporary presence here. Due to the similarity between the hairy flower of the edelweiss and the paw of a lion it is sometimes called Lion's Foot.

Forget-me-not. This pretty flower is associated with sorrow and despairing love. We are told in a Danubian legend of a young man who was walking by the riverside with his sweetheart, when she began to admire some blue flowers she saw growing on an island in mid-stream. Recklessly the youth plunged into the water and gathered the flowers, regardless of the icy cold. When close to the bank with the flowers clutched in his hand he was suddenly swept downstream by the current, but with his last strength he flung the flowers to his lady, crying out, "Forget me not." Until her dying day the girl wore the flowers in her hair in memory of his self-sacrificing, even foolish, love.

In an old Biblical tradition Adam, when naming the plants in Eden, overlooked one of them because of its minuteness. As he passed it he was suddenly interrupted by a very small voice which asked, "By what name am I called, Adam?" To which the embarrassed Adam replied with great resourcefulness, "You shall be my forget-me-not."

Geranium. There is a Middle Eastern legend which explains how the first geranium came into being. After the prophet Mahomet had washed his shirt he hung it on a lavender mallow to dry. By the time the shirt was ready to wear the shrub had miraculously sprouted forth sweet-scented red flowers – the first geraniums in the world.

Hyacinth. The hyacinth is a plant of poetry. According to Greek legend it sprang out of the blood of Hyacinthus, a Laconian youth who was inadvertently killed by a quoit thrown by Phoebus the sun god. The Jesuit poet Rapin refers to the flower thus:

> If spring prove mild 'tis hyacinthus time
> A flower which also rose from Phoebus' crime.

Homer says that the couch of Jupiter and Juno was decked with hyacinths, among other flowers:

> Thick new-born violets a soft carpet spread
> And clustering lotus swelled the rising bed.
> And suddenly hyacinths the turf bestrow
> And flowery crocus made the mountains grow.

Iris, the flower named after the goddess Iris, is the deity of the rainbow. It was she who guided the souls of women to their final resting-place in the other world, wherefore ancient Greeks planted irises on graves. Louis VII of France once dreamed of the flower and was so impressed that he adopted it as his device when fighting in the Crusades. From then onwards the iris became famous in France firstly as the fleur-de-Louis, then fleur-de-luce, and finally in its modern form, fleur-de-lis. This emblem was quartered by King Edward III with the cross of England, and appeared in the English heraldic shield until its removal at the beginning of the nineteenth century, at the time of the wars with France. The three leaves of the iris symbolize faith, wisdom and valour. The yellow iris is the flower honoured in this remarkable fashion by history. The more gaudily painted varieties, particularly those of mixed tints, have been likened to the rainbow which appears in the sky after a storm. For this reason the Greeks chose the Iris as the messenger and emblem of the gods.

Ivy. A garland of ivy in flower reminds us of winter's greyness and gloom, for in legend ivy, owls and ruins go together. Ivy clings romantically to crumbling castles, mouldering mansions and neglected tombs. Our ancestors tended to have mixed feelings about the ivy, considering there might possibly be some element of hope in a plant which bloomed when the remainder of the flower kingdom was dying or dead. Bunches of ivy leaves were attached to barn doors to keep away witches who in the old days were usually blamed for cattle diseases. And in that not so distant past, when people relied upon the flowers, leaves and herbs of the hedgerows for their medicines, herbalists mixed ivy-leaf cough mixtures for bronchial sufferers and ivy skin tonics for pimply persons. Strange to say, ivy provided a corn cure in Oxfordshire, a herb for sore eyes in Hertfordshire, and was also used as a shampoo.

A bunch of ivy kept inside the house indicated the shape of the future: if it flourished one might expect long life and happiness, but its withering was an omen of death. Lovelorn girls used ivy leaves as a magical charm to discover whom they would marry. If a girl carried a sprig of ivy in her pocket the first man she met was destined to be her husband.

One of the most important standbys of the old-time English drunkard was, strange to say, the ivy which was supposed to have the supernatural power to neutralize the effects of alcohol. Wearing a crown of ivy leaves prevented a hangover, and stopped the hair from falling out. Heavy drinkers actually drank their wine from cups made from ivy wood. In old English country fairs the drinking tents were decorated with bushes of ivy to show that good wine was sold inside. Early in history the ivy bush became an inn sign and this is the very odd reason for that very old saying, "A good wine needs no bush." All this becomes intelligible when we remember that Bacchus, the Roman god of wine, was crowned with a garland of ivy leaves.

Wine and Ivy Leaves

Jasmine is known in India as The Moonlight of the Grove. This flower is a frequent theme in the poetry of the East. It is one of the sacred flowers in India and Persia; and in China is an emblem of beauty. Among Christians the star-shaped blossoms mean heavenly felicity. According to legend many of the world's most beautiful flowers died on the night of the Crucifixion overwhelmed with grief, but the jasmine, which was originally pink, folded its leaves and bore its sufferings stoically, despite the fact that its name means in Arabic "despair and illusion". By morning it was obvious that the flower had lost its original colour and turned a ghastly pale, and so it has remained from that time forth. As a love symbol jasmine promises deep affection, and for this reason it is incorporated among the flowers of Indian bridal wreaths.

The *Lilac*, which had its original home in Persia, derives its name from the Persian *lilag*, meaning flower. Purple lilac was at one time the colour of mourning and presenting a spray of the flowers to a lover was a sensitive way of indicating that the romance had died. There is an American superstition that a girl who wears lilac is destined to remain unmarried. This was inspired by the story of the English nobleman who seduced an innocent girl and abandoned her, leaving her to die of a broken heart. Her friends laid a wreath of purple lilacs upon her grave, but overnight each blossom was transformed into a white flower, the symbol of innocence and, as the reader will be aware, of mourning.

Lily. According to an ancient Christian legend the first lily "sprang from the tears of Eve as she went forth from Eden". However, long before Christianity the white lily was held in the highest esteem by the Greeks and Romans, and was one of the flowers incorporated in the couch of Juno and Jupiter. Later in history the lily was assigned to the Madonna whose emblem it remains today. The sceptical St Thomas, who expressed doubts as to whether the Virgin had been resurrected, had her tomb opened only to find it filled with beautiful roses and white lilies. Diana, Juno and Lilith, Adam's first wife, wore lilies as their emblems. Lilies lie under the dominion of Mars.

Lily of the Valley. The divine patroness of the lily of the valley was Ostara, the Norse goddess of springtime. In English folklore we find the legend of battle fought between St Leonard and a hor-

The Dragon in the Wood

rifying dragon named Sin. The combat raged for three days with honours about even, but on the fourth day virtue overcame evil and the monster conceded defeat, creeping off into the woods to lick its wounds. Alas the saint had suffered grievous injury, and wherever his blood had dripped to the earth there grew a lily of the valley.

Lotus. This is one of the most interesting flowers known to man, deriving its name from Lotis, Neptune's beautiful daughter who was transformed into a lotus tree by the gods to safeguard her from the obscene caresses of Priapus, the Greek personification of male sexual power. According to Homer, any person who ate the fruit of the lotus lost all sense of the world around him, forgetting its troubles and its cares.

> And those who tasted of their flowery meat
> Cared not with tidings to return but clave
> First to that tribe, for ever fain to eat –
> Reckless of home return – the tender lotos sweet.
>
> From the *Odyssey*

Marigold. This flower spells jealousy, being a symbol of cruelty in love and unhappiness. It has been endowed by country folk with a wide variety of names: the bride of the sun, the golden flower, death flower, and water dragon. In a legend told by the Greeks to account for its origins (which have much in common with floral creation myths in general), we are told how a Greek girl named Caltha fell in love with the sun god, but was melted by his rays and in her place grew a solitary marigold.

The Mexicans say that the scarlet marigold bears the imprint of the blood of the Aztecs murdered by the Spaniards in their merciless quest for gold. The flower has an unlucky reputation in Germany where young women are warned against using it to divine the future.

Mignonette. This flower, known as the "little darling", derives its principal charm from its perfume. It is a tranquil plant, indeed its secondary name sweet reseda means "to soothe". It is also the emblem of good health, modesty and love. The mignonette originated in Egypt and was introduced into England from France where it is called *herbe d'amour* (love flower).

Mimosa. This, one of the most sensitive of plants, is related to the Egyptian mimosa from which comes the gum frankincense.

There is an old tradition that should a sinner pass a mimosa it folds its leaves with horror. The ancient Greeks believed the mimosa to be the metamorphosis of a delicate maid named Cephisa, who was given this shape so that she could escape from the embraces of Pan. The mimosa is a magical charm and in India a sprig is suspended above the bed or worn attached to the turban as an antidote to witchcraft and the evil eye.

Moss-rose. The moss-rose, one of the flowers of divination, is believed to have received its "veil of moss" as the gift of an angel. Country girls regarded any fading of the crimson hue of the petals as a sign that their lovers had ceased to care for them, as we find in an old poem "The Cottage Girl":

When faded, in its altered hue
She reads – the rustic is untrue.
But if it leaves the crimson paint
Her sickening hopes no longer faint.
The rose upon her bosom worn,
She meets him at the peep of morn.

Myrtle. The legends associated with the myrtle fall into the accustomed pattern. The flower was once a Greek maiden named Myrene, or alternatively the metamorphosis of Mirtilus, son of Mercury, the messenger of the gods. The myrtle has been described poetically as belonging to "the celestial race" of flowers.

Hence in Elysian Fields are Myrtles said
To favour lovers with their friendly shade.

When myrtle occurs in a dream it is a sign of good fortune, prosperity, a large family, and a ripe old age.

Due to its perennial greenness myrtle was regarded by the Greeks as an emblem of immortality and was worn as a garland by the high priest, by the initiates at the Eleusinian mysteries and by producers of plays and epics. A huge wreath of myrtle some ten feet in diameter was borne by those participating in the procession of Europa at Corinth. It is said that the custom of crowning individuals with myrtle originated with the Romans. The Arabs consider the myrtle to be the visible symbol of Allah's bounty. On their expulsion from Paradise, Adam and Eve were permitted to bring with them the most important foods and flowers: these were the date, which is the chief of fruits, and the myrtle which is pre-eminent among scented flowers.

There is a cheerless Greek superstition that anyone who passes a myrtle tree without picking one of the flowers is marked for death.

Narcissus. The white narcissus owes its name to one of the best known classical legends – to the youth Narcissus of whom it had been prophesied that he would live a long and happy life until the day he beheld the beauty of his own face. One day Narcissus chanced to glance at his reflection whilst quenching his thirst in a stream and, falling in love with his beauty, became transfixed to the spot where he gradually pined to death. In Ovid's poem we read how the flower which bears his name sprang from the body of the dead youth:

> And now the sister nymphs prepare his urn;
> When looking for his corpse, they only found
> A rising stalk with yellow blossoms crowned.

At the centre of this flower is a cup which tradition avers contains the tears of the dead Narcissus.

Nasturtium. According to the seventeenth-century Jesuit poet Rapin who retold the classical legends in his *De Hortorum Cultura,* the nasturtium was the metamorphosis of a Trojan huntsman, but of this curious legend nothing more is remembered. The seeds are reputed to have a supernatural power to repel serpents, while the flowers are supposed to sparkle at night. English flower lovers called it the yellow lark's heel. The nasturtium is the floral symbol of patriotism, and the scarlet variety symbolizes "splendour".

Oleander, known in England as the rose bay and laurel rose, is almost universally regarded as a plant of evil because of its "funereal and sickly character". The Tuscans, Sicilians and peoples of India employ the flowers at funerals. There is, however, a curious legend from Spain which offers a happier aspect. It tells how a young girl, when at death's door from a fever, was miraculously restored to health by St Joseph who materialized carrying a flowering oleander which he placed on the sick child's breast. From that moment the girl began to recover and the oleander became inevitably the flower of St Joseph.

Orchis. This flower is the metamorphosis of Orchis, the sacrilegious and wanton son of the satyr Pattelanus and the nymph Acolasia, who was torn to pieces by furious Bucchanals after he had assaulted one of their priestesses. His mangled body was afterwards transformed into the flower which bears his name, not as an act of grace but as a reminder to future generations of his impious behaviour.

According to an English tradition of a very different character, the purple spots staining the leaves of the orchis represent drops of blood which fell from Christ's body at the Crucifixion. In Northern Europe the sweet-scented orchis was associated with the Norse goddess Frigga, wife of Odin, helper of mankind and deity of maternal love and marriage.

The *Pansy*, or heart's-ease, derives its name from *pensées* meaning "thoughts" and is referred to by the Jesuit poet Rapin as The Flower of Jove. The poet Robert Herrick tells how it originated:

> Frolick virgins once there were
> Ever loving, living there
> Being here, their ends denied.
> Ran for sweethearts mad, and died.
> Love, in pity of their tears,
> And their loss in blooming years,
> For their restless here-spent hours
> Gave them Heart's-Ease, turned to flowers.

Under its English name heart's-ease, the pansy is sacred to St Valentine and therefore to lovers, and is also known to country folk as love-in-idleness.

The *Passion-Flower* is associated with a number of interesting legends, all of ancient lineage. According to the Spaniards this was the flower which climbed Christ's cross attaching itself to the holes made by the nails. Another early legend associated five different features of the flower with the wounds of Christ: the hammer, the spear, the pillar where He was scourged, the nails, and the crown of thorns. So closely was the passion-flower identified with the Christian ideal that the Spanish invaders of South America who discovered it growing there assumed that its presence was a clear indication that God intended the natives to become ready converts to Christianity. This provoked the following comment from a religiously-minded botanist: "I dare say God never willed His priests to instruct His people with lies: for they come from the Devil, the author of them."

The passion-flower is highly favoured as a symbol by workers in stained glass and iron and religious decoration generally where it has sometimes been employed to the exclusion of other floral symbols.

Peony. Once again we find in the peony, as with so many other plants and flowers, curious links with classical legend. It is said to have been the first plant employed as a healing agent, indeed the poet Homer declares that the name was adapted from Paeon who cured Pluto, god of the Underworld. The Greeks regarded the peony as a sacred flower with the power to keep evil spirits at bay.

The peony is highly favoured by the Chinese, who call it Moutan, and use it as a motif in the decoration of temple walls. We learn from a curious Chinese legend, with undertones of the demon lover of European mythology, how a scholar fell passionately in love with a beautiful and talented woman. However, on discovering that an important Chinese moralist was on his way to the scene she departed in great haste saying: "I am not a human creature, I am the soul of a peony. Your love warmed me into human shape – but now I must return to the flowers." And so saying her figure became wraithlike and gradually faded into the wall.

Pimpernel. The scarlet pimpernel, known as the Poor Man's Weather Glass, is one of those curious floral barometers we find in our gardens, for it closes its petals before and during rain. It also serves as a time-piece, opening its petals at seven a.m. and closing them again at siesta time, around two p.m. The pimpernel is in fact a plant of many qualities, medicinal as well as magical, which is well expressed in the lines:

> No ear hath heard
> No tongue can tell
> The virtues of the pimpernel.

The pimpernel is stained scarlet with the blood of Jesus Christ, according to Christian mythology.

The *Poppy,* once regarded as a symbol of death due to its bloody hue, was confirmed in this fatal role when the son of Tarquinus Superbus slashed off poppy heads in a garden as a signal to commence the massacre of the population of a conquered city.

It was because the poppy grew in cornfields that the ancients dedicated it to Ceres the Corn Goddess, who is invariably portrayed with poppies in her hair. The red poppy is closely associated with the concept of death and war. After the Battle of Neerwinden the meadows were scarlet with poppies, as were later in history the fields of Flanders. There is a superstition that the red poppies which grew on the battlefield of Waterloo sprang from the blood of the men who died there. Astrologers say the poppy is a flower of the moon.

The *Primrose* sprang from the body of a handsome youth called Paralisos (which is the ancient name of this pretty flower) after he had died of a broken heart following the loss of his sweetheart. The Germans had a tradition that carrying a primrose provided an "Open Sesame" to hidden treasures, hence its folk name the Key Flower.

Rose. We are indebted to the Jesuit poet René Rapin for the story of the origins of the rose. The flower was originally a Grecian Queen whose beauty excited the jealousy of the goddess Diana. Phoebus the sun god, the brother of Diana, then scorched the maid with his fiery rays until she was reduced to the beautiful flower of our gardens. Her three lovers who had pursued her to the temple of Diana were also punished, being transformed into a butterfly, a worm and a drone, respectively.

Apuleius relates in his *Golden Ass* a tale in which a young man was transformed into an ass, and to regain his human shape had to discover and eat a rose. He performed the task set him, and after many tribulations recovered his humanity.

To the ancient Greeks the rose was the emblem of Venus, its fragrance Cupid's gift. Red roses were the flowers of Adonis, white roses the emblems of the moon. In the language of love the red rose represents love and the white silence, while red and white roses combined symbolize unity.

Cleopatra poured out half Egypt's wealth on roses for the feast she gave in honour of her lover Mark Antony. Roman brides wore garlands of roses on their wedding day. Roses came to England with the Romans who scattered petals upon the graves of dead lovers, and planted red and white roses on their tombs. Love and death walked hand-in-hand in the gardens of England during the Wars of the Roses, when the partisans of the red and white rose fought so bitterly for the Crown. Out of that carnage came the emblem of national union – the Rose of England, the Tudor Rose.

A secret society of Rosicrucians comprised of mystical philosophers and alchemists was founded by Christian Rosenkreuz in the fifteenth century. It is mentioned by Samuel Butler in his *Hudibras,* thus

> As for the Rosycross philosophers
> Whom you will have to be but sorcerers . . .

Their symbol, a rose surmounted on a cross – which has puzzled students of the occult for centuries, could well have been inspired by the name of the founder or have arisen because the rose is a symbol of secrecy.

Rose lovers will be delighted to learn that their favourite flowers were at one time highly valued for their medicinal qualities. This tradition can be traced to the classical legend of the maid Milto who rendered a daily offering of roses to the goddess Venus and was rewarded by being healed of a tumour on her chin. Cyrus, King of Persia, was so smitten by the maiden's beauty that he made her his wife.

The Persians say that a nightingale began to sing when the roses first bloomed and then, overcome by the perfume, fell to the earth where his blood spilled upon the petals transforming them miraculously from white to crimson.

Rosemary. A bizarre legend is associated with rosemary, which is also known as Dew of Sea because of its prevalence in coastal areas. A certain Queen of Italy gave birth to a rosemary bush which was stolen from her by a King of Spain. One day the King, while playing his flute, saw to his amazement a beautiful princess emerging from the bush. He fell in love with her and on his departure for the wars left the bush in the care of his head gardener. However, the King's sisters while playing their flutes near the bush saw the maiden and, smitten by jealousy, struck her. The princess vanished and the bush wilted; it could only be revived with dragon's blood. And so the gardener ventured out in pursuit of a dragon, hoping to procure some dragon's blood with which to bring the bush back to life before the King's return. This he was at last able to do. On his return from the wars, the King wed the rose-maiden whose name was Rosa Marina, and everybody lived happily ever after.

The *Snowdrop,* also known as the Fair Maid of February, had its legendary origins in Biblical mythology, with the expulsion of Adam and Eve from the Garden of Eden. As Eve stood mournfully surveying the barren earth around her which was not only flowerless but white with snow, an angel suddenly appeared and, catching a snowflake breathed upon it, and handing it to her said:

> This is an earnest, Eve to thee
> That sun and summer soon shall be.

She vanished and in her place there grew a ring of snowdrops. In traditional legend the snowflake is the emblem of purity.

Speedwell or Veronica. The speedwell is so named because its corolla falls and is borne away on the wind. Among the women who followed Jesus Christ on His agonized journey to Calvary was the compassionate Veronica (afterwards beatified) who held her handkerchief against His face. Miraculously the likeness of Jesus Christ was transferred to the cloth.

Star of Bethlehem. The white stellate flowers of this plant which grows in Samaria are reminiscent of the star which illuminated the Heavens immediately above the birthplace of Jesus Christ. This flower is of the horological variety, unfolding its petals around eleven a.m., hence its popular name Eleven O'Clock Lady. The French have a legend describing how the Star of Bethlehem was discovered among the grasses upon which the infant Christ lay in His manger.

Stock or Gillyflower. "The white and purple gillyflowers that stay/In blossom, lingering Summer half away" were among the first garden flowers to be cultivated in England, and were also reputed to have grown in Paradise. The gillyflower is the symbol of "unfading beauty".

Sunflower. Its legendary origins are described in the following legend. Clytie, a beautiful water nymph, fell in love with the sun god Apollo but found him completely unresponsive since he was enamoured with Caliope, the muse of epic poetry. So, brokenhearted, Clytie pined away and died of melancholy, her limbs slowly dissolving into the earth where they took root, while her body was transformed into a slender stem, and her face into the sunflower.

The movements of the sunflower have aroused much scholarly comment over the ages. Hyll says in his sixteenth-century book *The Art of Gardening*: "After the rising of the sun into noon this flower openeth larger and larger; but after the noon-time into the setting of the sun, the flowers closeth more and more, so that after the setting thereof it is wholly shut up." The poet James Thomson reaffirms this view:

> The lofty follower of the sun,
> Sad when he sets, shuts up her yellow leaves,
> Drooping all night, and when he warm returns
> Points her enamoured bosom to his rays.
>
> From *The Seasons*

Tulip. It is obvious from the legends inherited from classical times that flowers were of immense significance to the early civilizations. Time and time again we return to the theme that a particular blossom derived either its characteristics or its name from some hapless maiden who was metamorphosed into a plant whilst eluding the caresses of an ogre or satyr or god. So we have the story of the Dalmatian nymph who was transformed into a tulip to protect her from the unwanted embraces of Vertumnus, the Roman god of the seasons. From that time onwards, so the poet Rapin says:

> The face and ribbons that adorned the fair
> To leaves are changed; her breast a stem is made,
> Slender and long with fragrant greens arrayed;
> Six gaudy leaves a painted cup compose,
> On which kind nature every dye bestows;
> For though the nymph transformed, the love she bore
> To colours still delight her as before.

Tulips acquired an incredible importance in Holland in the seventeenth century where they became cult objects among rich and poor alike and were even quoted as assets by those seeking a loan. Tulips which were at first novelties rapidly became status symbols; if you were minus your tulip you became, socially speaking, an outsider. Prices of tulips began to rise, then rocketed, until almost overnight Holland became the centre of the maddest mania ever known – tulipmania. Flowers sold for as much as 4,000 guilders for a single bulb while a clutch of 120 went for nearly 100,000 florins. People invested their entire fortunes in tulips and there was a dreadful tale told of an Amsterdam man who absent-mindedly ate a vast fortune in tulips, having confused them with spring onions.

Tulipmania spread to Britain where the bulbs were actually quoted on the Stock Exchange, although never reaching the fantastic prices of Amsterdam. At first they sold at a few guineas apiece and later for as much as fifteen guineas. In the nineteenth century more and more Londoners became bitten by tulipmania, and in 1835 a single bulb was auctioned for £35. Greater love hath no man than he who gives his life for his flowers. It was, in fact, an English florist who, on a frosty night in 1849, covered his tulip beds with his own blanket and caught a cold and died – of tulipmania.

Violet. Like the tulip the violet began its existence as a nymph who was transformed into a flower to secure her virginity from a rapacious god, in this case Phoebus, the sun deity. The violet was one of the flowers dedicated to Diana, goddess of the crescent moon, "to whom all flowers growing in untrodden dells uncontaminated by the tread of men, especially belonged". Strange to say, if violets bloom at the fall of the leaf an illness can be expected.

Wallflower. Tradition ascribes a poetic origin to the wallflower, dating to the ages of chivalry. A maiden who had been imprisoned in a Scottish castle attempted to escape and join her lover who, disguised as a troubadour, waited outside the walls. Alas, she fell to the ground and died before her lover's eyes, only to be reborn as a flower. The tragedy inspired Robert Herrick's lines:

> Love in pity of the deed,
> And her loving luckless speed
> Turned her to this plant we call
> Now the Flower of the Wall.

The wallflower symbolizes fidelity in adversity.

Water-lilies. The German peasants believed that the water nymphs disguised themselves as water-lilies when harried by lustful males. Understandably, therefore, this flower became a symbol of chastity, so much so that in the Middle Ages when the love potion was employed to overcome maidenly scruples, a lady could resist its magical influence by carrying one of the blossoms in her hand. In the Far East it was customary for mourners to carry water-lilies at funeral ceremonies as a testimony to the virtue of the deceased.

CHAPTER SEVEN

The Magic of Perfume

Perfume has been associated throughout history with sexual attraction, but it is obvious from the word itself which means "through the smoke" that it was at one time connected with fire. In fact, aromatic herbs, flowers and woods were burned in antiquity within temples as fumigants and to give pleasure to the gods when sacrifices were made. The scent of exotic flowers was supposed to ascend to regions beyond the temple ceilings to the Heavens where they perfumed the realms of Paradise. In many places even today flower scents are thought to have supernatural qualities. South Sea Islanders believe that the scent is "the spirit of the flower".

Turning back the pages of time we discover that in the barbaric and in some ways beautiful rituals of the past the vast majority of the raw materials of the sacrifice was supplied by flowers, some of which were imported at great expense from far-off countries. Myrrh had its origins in Ethiopia, being one of the precious gifts brought by the Magi to the Infant Christ. Sandalwood, one of the best known of the perfumed woods of the East, was employed in the construction of the sacred images in the temples. Other precious flowers, for example the tuberose, which was known as the Mistress of the Night since no woman could resist its seductive power, came from as far afield as Malaya.

The Canticles indicate the influence of perfume among the Jews: "While the king sitteth at his table my spikenard sendeth forth the smell thereof." "Who is this that cometh out of the wilderness like pillars of smoke perfumed with myrrh and frankincense with all the powders of the merchant." "The plants are an orchard of pomegranates with pleasant fruits; camphire with spikenard; spikenard and saffron, myrrh and aloes, calamus and cinnamon with all the chief spices." Camphire, a fragrant flower, was used to perfume rooms and was also worn garlanded around the neck. Saffron was the product of the dried stigma of the crocus. The ancient Egyptians, like modern Europeans, used perfumes extensively in courtship. Queen Cleopatra's royal barge is known to have wafted the most exotic scents on the winds as it progressed down the Nile on the journey to meet Mark Antony.

The perfumer's art developed rapidly in Mediterranean lands, particularly in ancient Greece where every private house possessed its altar from which delicate essences were sent soaring heavenwards to satisfy the aesthetic senses of the gods. The passion for floral perfumes is referred to by Philoxenus in his play *The Banquet*:

And then the slaves brought water for the hands,
And soap well mixed with juicy oil of lilies,
And pour'd o'er the hands as much warm water
As the guests wish'd. And then they gave them towels
Of finest linen, beautifully wrought,
And fragrant ointments of ambrosial smell,
And garlands of the flowering violet.

The rose was one of the flowers most favoured by the Arabs for Mahomet had said: "When I was taken up to heaven some of my sweat fell on the earth and from it sprang the rose, and whoever would smell my scent, let him smell the rose." In the Middle East a guest or stranger would be welcomed into the home with a sprinkling of rose-water, a custom mentioned by Byron in "The Bride of Abydos" (the word *gul* means rose):

She snatched the urn wherein was mix'd
The Persian Atar-gul's perfume
And sprinkled all its odours o'er
The pictur'd roof and marble floor.

The Crusaders returning from the Holy Land laden with the spoils of war brought with them the subtle perfumes of the Orient, greatly to the alarm of the medieval clergy who had a tendency to associate scent with Satanism.

Washing the skin remained one of the lost arts of civilization as late as the Tudor period, when even those belonging to the highest strata of society were content to apply aromatics to their bodies and clothing. Water seems to have been regarded by all classes with unimaginable horror, but the minority who were prepared to bathe favoured dilutions of rose-water and scented wash-balls in lieu of soap which had yet to be invented. In Queen Elizabeth's court perfumed gloves were the rage and later a glove perfume distilled from orange flowers became popular among the rich.

Among favourite English perfumes we find one called Spring-flowers which had a violet and rose base. Its ingredients were kept a close secret and remain so to this day. The formula for one of those exotic glove perfumes has survived however, and consists of coriander seeds, rosewood and lavender combined with benzoin, storax, calamus, citron essence and rose petals.

The herbalist Gerard described the rose as holding "the chiefest and most principal place among all flowers whatsoever being not only greatly esteemed for his bountie virtues and his fragrant smell but because it is the honour and virtue of our English sceptre."

In times past one of the little recorded activities of our monarchs was the preparation of floral perfumes. One famous expert, Queen Elizabeth I, possessed her own still room. Queen Anne had a perfume prepared by her confectioner who had studied the art to perfection. It was called Royal Perfume and the recipe is as follows: "Take three spoonfuls of perfect rosemary and as much sugar as half a walnut beaten into small powder; all these boyle together in a perfuming-pan upon hot embers with a few coals."

One of the most remarkable demonstrations of the use of flowers for amorous ends was provided by James Graham, an eighteenth-century English quack doctor and eccentric who offered the use of a miraculous bed for a consideration to couples desirous of child-bearing. This bed was advertised as emanating "magical influences which are now celebrated from Pole to Pole, and from the rising to the setting sun." To ensure a successful outcome for its users the bed was surmounted by a dome-like structure which emanated "odoriferous and balmy spells, odours and essences which are exhaled by the breath of music by the exhilarating force of electric power." The mattress was stuffed with stallion's hair, and sweet new wheat and outstraw, mingled with balm, rose leaves, lavender flowers and oriental spices. Tudor roses perfumed the sheets of this truly remarkable bed.

In an endeavour to rationalize the mystique surrounding scents, a scholar once produced a scale of the eighteen primary floral perfumes:

1 The Rose series	7 Spice	13 Mint
2 Jasmine	8 Clove	14 Anise
3 Orange flower	9 Camphor	15 Almond
4 Tuberose	10 Sandalwood	16 Musk
5 Violet	11 Citrine	17 Amber
6 Vanilla	12 Lavender	18 Fruit

As Daphne Barraclough says in her fascinating book *A Flower-Lover's Miscellany*: "There must be few flower lovers who have not at some time or other longed to capture forever, the fragrance of some particular blossom: the sharp-sweetness of the lily of the valley on a May morning, the haunting perfume of tobacco flowers in the dusk of a summer's eve. . . ."

The seventeenth-century diarist John Evelyn would have echoed these delightful sentiments, for he recommended to King Charles II the establishment of plantations "such as yield the most sweet smelling flowers". However, the path of the floral perfumer was not always strewn with rose petals, for we find during the following century opposition arising, the House of Commons giving serious consideration to the application of the laws against witchcraft to any woman who attempted "to seduce into matrimony one of his Majesty's subjects by the aid of scent". One can appreciate the alarm felt by wealthy bachelors at the approach of the seductress heavy with the fragrance of lily of the valley on a May morning. It is a well-known fact that perfumes, and more especially incenses, were used in magical ceremonies in order to heighten perception. Liquid incenses were most commonly used by magicians, and were distilled in complete darkness since light was supposed to have a deleterious effect upon them. The oil thus produced was first poured into a metal pan and then ignited, while the magician muttered the mystical word *Tetragrammaton* and with thumbs locked extended his hands above the flames. Each ceremony demanded its own individual incense, its special floral or wood base. We find in old works of magic formulae for Ceremonial Incenses, Mystic Rites Incenses, Temple Incenses and Lovers' Incenses.

Old legends about incense inform us that incenses integrate the personality and dispel evil influences. Lovers' Incense had to be burned on the night of the full moon, in a gold burner which was free of any taint of dirt. A similar incense called Attraction Incense was credited with the power "to sweep the mind with pleasing thoughts".

From love incenses we turn to love divination, love philtres or aphrodisiacs (many based on floral preparations), which seem to have reached their highest peak of development in the ancient East and were later adopted with zest by lovers and would-be lovers in Greece and Rome.

Theocritus mentions the petal of the flower of a pepper tree called the telephilon which was placed before a fire and its reaction carefully studied. According to the reaction of its leaf under the heat the observer was able to judge whether or not his love would be returned.

Shakespeare refers in *Othello* to the lurking fear inspired by the use of love charms and aphrodisiacs in the sixteenth century:

> . . . what drugs, what charms,
> What conjuration, and what mighty magic . . .
>
> . . . thou hast practis'd on her with foul charms,
> Abus'd her delicate youth with drugs or minerals
> That weaken motion . . .

While it would be unwise to set down the various formulae in detail in case they proved lethal to the experimenter, it is safe to say that many common flowers had a vital function in love magic. Elecampane seeds, the flowers of vervain and mistletoe berries were among the ingredients favoured by magicians of the Tudor period; they also held the roots of sea holly in high regard. The potions were sweetened with sugar and eaten as sweets. Louis de Claremont recommends an apparently safe love cordial, for which this writer assumes no responsibility: "The flowers and leaves of myrtle, two handfulls, infuse them in two quarts of spring water and a quart of white wine, twenty-four hours, and then distil them in a cold still and this will be of a strong scent and

Floral Incenses

tincture, and by adding more or less of the myrtle you make it stronger or weaker as you please. This beautifies, and mixed with cordial syrups is a good cordial and inclines those that drink it to be very amorous."

Another exotic perfume with highly recommended erotic powers was Angel Water, a concoction of orange flower water, rose-water and myrtle water, distilled spirit of musk with ambergris which had to be carefully kept at a moderate temperature if it was not to exhaust its powers. And there was a Spring Nosegay based on hyacinths, violets, wallflowers, jonquils, Florentine orris, mace and quintessence of orange.

Those great adepts in the ancient art of love, the Hindus, gave special prominence to the jasmine, the lotus, and the asoka plant in prescriptions "to provoke venery". Although mandragora (or mandrake) is a Middle Eastern plant having no place among the roses of the traditional English garden, it has too important a role in plant magic to be excluded from any discussion of aphrodisiacs. According to that great authority on oriental matters, Sir Edwin Arnold, the mandrake "will renovate and re-invigorate falling bodily powers beyond all other stimulants".

Theophrastus believed the plant satyrion (*Orchis mascula*) to be more dynamic for it enabled its user to "accomplish the act of love twelve times successively".

There can be little doubt that the influence of such preparations dominated the ages of romance, but belief in the power of love magic is far from dead today and remains strong in the United States – especially among the poorer elements of the population.

In a recently published catalogue of "magical aids", which includes witchcraft regalia and grimoires of all kinds, there are advertisements for love powders and perfumed oils to which the advertiser prefaces the rider: "Some of the brand names are taken from legend and folklore. No claims or inferences are made for these perfumed oils having any supernatural powers." The list incorporates acacia, apple blossom, cactus, carnation, cloves, coriander, cumin seed, cypress, elm, French lilac, gardenia, geranium, heliotrope, honeysuckle, iris, jacinthe, jasmine, jungle gardenia, lavender, lilac, lily of the valley, love herbs, magnolia, mandrake, mint, musk, myrrh, myrtle, narcisse, orange blossom, pine, rosemary, rue, saffron, sandalwood, verbena, vervain, violet, white rose, wistaria, wormwood.

The uses of botanical essences and perfumes is very wide; they include the anointment of prelates, priests and kings. In ancient times even the royal dead were anointed with sandal-paste oil, this being the product of a sacred tree.

The magical influence of perfume cannot be denied, yet it remains an unsolved mystery. By its aid we recreate images of lovers long dead, and incidents buried by time. We are told by psychiatrists that uttering the name of a particular perfume can bring about the sensation of having smelt it.

Flower lovers need not be parted from perfume merely because their flowers have perished with the close of summer. *Pot-pourri* ensures that the garden lives on through the winter, exciting the imagination with images of flowers which can no longer delight the eye.

Pot-pourri is the French translation of *olla podrida*, a Spanish dish prepared from a miscellany of meats and vegetables, minced and stewed. It later came to mean any kind of hotchpotch musical and literary composition, and then in turn a mixture of dried flower petals, principally rose or lavender, preserved for their fragrance in a china jar. There are a number of major "themes" in *pot-pourri*, for example the exotic Verbena, Mystic East, and Summertime *pot-pourris*, the latter comprising rose petals, lavender flowers, carnation petals, marigold petals, pinks and stocks, all readily obtainable from the flower garden.

Blends of *pot-pourri* are also used to fill sachets and are particularly pleasing if left in cupboards and drawers where they introduce a breath of sunshine into the most wintry corners of the home. A curious old recipe includes an interesting *pot-pourri* "Sweet Pot" borrowed from the first quarter of the nineteenth century: "Put into a large china jar the following ingredients in layers with Bay Salt strewn between each layer: 2 picks Damask roses, part in bud and part flower; Violets, Orange flowers and Jasmine 1 handful each; Oris root shred, Benjamin and Storax 2 oz of each; ¼ oz of musk; ¼ lb Angelica root shred; A quart of the red parts of Clove, Gillyflowers; 2 handfuls of Lavender; Bay and Laurel leaves ½ handful of each; 3 Seville Oranges stuck as full of cloves as possible dried in a cool oven and pounded; ½ a handful of knotted Marjoram; 2 handfuls of Balm of Gilead."

It would be erroneous to presume that the brightest and most attractive flowers possess the most appealing perfumes, for the modest weed-like mignonette can perfume an entire garden with its beautiful and refreshing scent. There are, alas, many who are allergic to flowers. In Sir James Smith's *Elements* the author complained that honeysuckles "affected him in the house with violent pains in the temples, soon followed by sickness and partial loss of recollection". The scent of the iris gave him nausea and suffocated him, while the white lily, lilac and Peruvian heliotrope almost poisoned him. He had known a man to be overcome by the presence of a single carnation which had fallen behind the furniture in a well-aired drawing-room. However, in fairness he conceded that "roses are universally acceptable and scarcely noxious to anybody".

CHAPTER EIGHT

Gardens of Delight

Gardens cannot exist without gardeners nor flowers without the dedication of flower lovers – and so it has been all down the ages. Gardening can be religion, art, music and poetry all in one. It has a universal appeal and has inspired all social ranks to set aside their daily cares and lose themselves in the ecstasy of contact with Mother Earth.

In their fascinating book *Gardens of Delight* Miles and John Hadfield tell us: "Fundamentally all gardening is the transference of a vision into a touchable and seeable reality . . ." a statement embodying an important truth since every gardener attempts, consciously or otherwise, to emulate the creator in planting the flowers of Paradise.

Whether our garden happens to be an Eden, a landed estate or a suburban patch, it is often the realization of a lifelong dream and an act of faith in the creative powers of nature. We join with Sir William Temple who wrote in his essay "Upon the Garden of Epicurus": "We must accept that God Almighty esteemed the life of man in a garden the happiest He could give."

As we have seen, classical writers believed beautiful flower gardens to have been the playgrounds of elemental spirits, otherwise sylphs and fauns. There was the Garden of Hesperides set on the very rim of the world, where grew the tree which bore the golden apple of fertility guarded by the nymphs Aegle, Arethusa, Erytheia, and Vesta. Then again there was the Garden of Ivem, created by Sheddad, King of Ad, which was intended to rival Eden but which disappeared at the touch of the wand carried by the Angel of Death.

Diodorus has recorded how Cyrus King of Persia created the Hanging Gardens of Babylon to give pleasure to his courtesan Amytis, who, coming from a mountainous country, desired only to be reminded of her home in the Median hills. The gardens, which were rectangular in shape and ascended in a series of terraces from the river, were regarded as one of the Seven Wonders of the Ancient World. The great Cyrus, despite his august majesty, did not restrict his activities to supervision but was prepared to delve the soil like any son of Adam. This is evident from his response to the compliments of Lysander, who, in lavishing praise upon the garden, diplomatically expressed his admiration of its presiding genius! ". . . but what strikes me most is the exquisite taste and elegant industry of the person who drew the plan of the several parts of this garden, and gave it the fine order, wonderful disposition, and happiness of symmetry, which I cannot sufficiently admire." To which Cyrus replied, "It was I that drew the plan, and entirely marked it out, and many of the trees which you see were planted with my own hands." Dilating further upon the pleasures of gardening Cyrus continued, much to Lysander's amazement, "I swear by the god Mithras, that when my health admits I never set down to table without having made myself sweat with some fatigue or other, either in military exercise, rural labour, or some other toilsome employment to which I apply with pleasure and without sparing myself."

This exuberant enthusiasm for gardening was by no means unique among the eminent men of antiquity. Following his abdication the Roman Emperor Diocletian devoted his entire leisure hours to the work of building, planting and gardening. When urged by his friends to resume the Imperial Purple and the irksome responsibilities of power, Diocletian avowed his preference for the cultivation of cabbages which gave him the kind of satisfaction he had never experienced as a statesman.

Even on the western side of the Atlantic there were gardens which inspired those who first saw them. According to Prescott, the Aztecs created miracles of horticulture – ". . . chinampas, or floating gardens – those wandering islands of verdure . . . teeming with flowers . . . and moving like rafts over the waters." The gardens of Iztapalapan were of immense size and beautified by creepers and aromatic shrubs which "loaded the air with perfumes". All these scenes of beauty had, alas, vanished within a generation, reduced by the Spanish conquest to "a foul and unsightly morass, the haunt of loathsome reptiles".

The ancient Aztecs held in high honour four maidens known respectively as The Goddess of Flowers, of Salt, of the Young Maize, and "Our Mother among the waters". They were the brides of Toxcatl, God of Gods, who, represented by a living man, was sacrificed annually in the month of April.

Among the curiosities of horticulture should be mentioned the Floating Gardens of Persia and Tibet which were constructed for the cultivation of melons, cucumbers and other plants requiring a very aqueous soil. These gardens were of a very fragile nature, "being composed of wickerwork, interlaced with reeds and watlings and covered with matting over which the earth is placed".

Turning to the civilization of Africa we find in Beechley's *Proceedings of an Expedition to Explore the Northern Coast of Africa* published early in the fifteenth century, the report of the discovery of strangely beautiful gardens in the neighbourhood of Benghazi beneath mighty rock cliffs. The gardens had been planted with fruit trees, the most exotic of which were compared by the author to "the far-famed garden of the Hesperides".

For the more exotic gardens it is necessary to journey to warmer climes, for the most interesting are in Japan. Japanese gardening was originally greatly influenced by the Chinese, but developed along its own highly individual lines protected by the isolationism long favoured by the Japanese state.

As early as the seventeenth century Englebert Kaempfer, a Dutch naturalist, put on record his impressions of the Japanese love of gardening in his *History of Japan*: "If there be not room enough for a garden they [the Japanese] have at least an old ingrafted plum, cherry or apricot tree. The older, the more crooked and monstrous the tree is, the greater value they put upon it. Sometimes they let the branches grow into the rooms. In order to make it bear larger flowers and in greater quantity, they commonly cut it to a few, perhaps two or three branches. It cannot be denied that the great number of beautiful, incarnate and double flowers which they bear in the proper Season, are a surprisingly curious ornament to this back part of the house. . . . Ordinary people often plant the same kind of trees before the

Floating Garden: Fruit and Flowers

street-doors, for their diversion as well as for an ornament to their houses."

Lafcadio Hearn, the author and poet who made his home among the Japanese at the close of the nineteenth century, professed himself fascinated by the beauty of the gardens, each with its ". . . miniature lake fringed with rare plants and containing a tiny island with tiny mountains and dwarf peach trees, and pines and azaleas . . ." In Japanese gardens flowers were suspended from the trees in pots with bells and little lighted lanterns as a testament to beauty and the national desire to worship it.

The gardens of China were secret places, from which barbarians and foreign devils were excluded. Robert Fortune, the first plant collector to visit China, was given the rare privilege of seeing the mysterious Gardens of the Mandarins with their beautiful ornamental trees and shrubs – a triumph indeed, for access was made incredibly difficult by the almost impenetrable wall of reserve which barred Chinese horticulture from foreign eyes.

William Kerr, the nineteenth-century son of a Scottish nurseryman, was received by the inhospitable Chinese with ". . . antagonism, uncooperativeness, an almost complete lack of facilities for travel and a people who almost spat at his shadow." Nevertheless, despite this hostility Kerr visited the famous Fa-tee Gardens – known as Flowery Land – where he marvelled at the fantastic blaze of colour which conveyed the impression that every brilliant blossom in the whole of China was displayed before his eyes. It was a terrestrial Eden, a floral paradise of azaleas, orange trees, roses, tree peonies and white gardenias, ". . . an Aladdin's cave of floral rarities such as no Westerner had seen before him."

English gardens did not come into their own until the sixteenth century, and prior to that time had been mainly confined to the monasteries where they were dedicated to the cultivation of fruit, vegetables and medicinal herbs for the use of the monks. There were, however, early references to flowers in the writings of one twelfth-century gardener: "The garden," he wrote, "should be adorned on this side with roses, lilies and the marigold; on that side with parsley, cost [an aromatic bark], fennel, southern wood, coriander, sages, savory, hyssop, vine. . . . The garden is also enriched by the cucumber, the soporiferous poppy and the

love in anyone of the opposite sex who strays within your charmed enclosure.

Now to the astral territory dedicated to Hermes, God of Mercury. You must first plant a lemon tree to act as the symbol of pleasant thoughts, since according to a very old belief this was the true tree of knowledge of good and evil in the Garden of Eden. We should include two other plants belonging to the mercurial planet, primulas and antirrhinums, for they endow the owner of the garden with happiness and good luck.

Next come the plants of Jupiter and purple flowers which are symbols of royalty, for example, purple violets and the purple buddleia which butterflies find irresistible. Butterflies, incidentally, are symbols of the soul, in contrast to worms which represent the corruptible body. Purple flowers confer regality upon every garden in which they grow for the colour is the emblem of honour, glory, dignity, trust and wisdom. Such blossoms bear all the attributes of the wise monarch although in its negative sense, purple can have an unfavourable aspect: overweening pride, arrogance and ostentation.

At this phase of the operation it becomes necessary to decide upon the appropriate days for planting the garden, a process which in all cases involves the propitiation of the supernatural powers. For thousands of years men and women have linked their fortunes to the moon and stars, believing it essential to commence cultivation at times when these luminaries were most favourable to the operation in hand. Farmers long believed that crops must be planted at the time of the waxing moon (that is, the period from new moon to the full moon), but destructive or negative work had to be deferred until the waning. This is the time for killing greenfly and similar pests, weeding and rooting up unwanted plants. However, it should not be taken for granted that weeds are necessarily plants of evil, for the philosophy of "eating the weeds" is now very much in vogue. Almost everything in nature has its good or positive aspect if one is sufficiently hungry, or so it appears.

The philosophy of planting with the planets was fully understood by the village herb women who dispensed remedies to the rural poor up to the middle of the nineteenth century when their medicines became outmoded. It is interesting to discover the extent to which their derided principles are not only becoming restored to fashion, but are proving correct.

The flowers of love are essential to all gardens where the power of magic is to be maintained. They include night-scented stocks, azaleas and orange blossom, all of which are linked with the sun and are therefore conveyors of fertility. It is a good idea to plant gypsophila, particularly the crimson variety as this is traditionally a flower of romance.

The writer Joan Stephens, in a fascinating article "The Magic Garden" admits that ". . . a garden planted by the planets sounds a bit patchy in colour but in practice it is not. The patches spread and overlap and all link up together to make a garden that has a strange and lovely occult atmosphere." Indeed, the atmospheric qualities of such a garden enable it to exert its maximum power over the imagination. The features that are most conducive to this artistry will be familiar: secluded arbors, shady groves, falling water and silent pools. Still water has an overpowering effect on the mind being a mirror of the soul, just as the eyes are its windows.

A fountain is necessary to complete the garden, for in terms of symbolism it represents the principles of erudition, healing and perpetual renewal of the emotional powers.

It is essential if your garden is to be properly attuned to nature to make provision for wild life. Among psychically helpful denizens of gardens are frogs and toads. Birds, butterflies and bees should also make their homes there if only to maintain the ancient principle that small flying creatures are agents of the celestial powers, in other words the winged messengers of the gods. To be completely up-to-date one should provide an area for the protection of species which, like spiritually directed human beings, are endangered by the ever-expanding urban desert with its hordes of unthinking vandals and unfeeling money maniacs.

As the booklet *Hertfordshire Wildlife* tells us: "Our gardens contain the biggest area that can be devoted to nature conservation in Britain today . . ." and ". . . what is more this land is private with resident game wardens." The author reminds us that limitations in ground area can be compensated by an "environment upwards" consisting of trees, hedges and climbing plants, which provide a chain of life ranging from insects, including caterpillars, to our cheerful garden birds.

A lawn makes an ideal landing strip for birds like starlings

The Living World

which delight to alight in huge aerial flotillas. Even a compost heap has its proper place in the skilfully contrived miniature wildlife park, for it is a refuge of the ever-popular hedgehog who will repay you with many summer visits at dusk, particularly when the weather is warm.

And don't forget the nesting boxes which should face either north or east, and remember that the pool or fountain provides a home for gracefully gliding fishes, those traditional symbols of wisdom the world over. The denizens of our gardens provide supernatural guidance in a number of important ways. Birds, for instance, can indicate to those with an observant eye what the future might have in store for the householder. To hear the call of a night bird in daytime is an unhappy omen as is a bird which taps on the window pane with its beak or enters the home via the chimney.

To injure a robin is considered unlucky, and there is an Oxfordshire superstition which says that a robin heard singing in the doorway is a sign of death. If on looking out of the windows onto your garden you see a flock of birds to your right it is an indication of a happy day ahead, but if on the left prepare for trouble. One could well describe garden birds as arboreal astrological almanacs. These ideas are very old indeed and can be traced to the soothsayers of ancient times who interpreted the future by studying the behaviour of birds.

Bees are invariably luck-bringers and were believed in ancient times to have originated in Paradise. There is still a superstition that a bond of sympathy exists between the people in the house and the bees in the hive. Some country-folk say that unless the bees are told of every important household event they will either fly away or die. At weddings the hives are sometimes decked with white ribbons and at funerals with black crêpe. Butterflies also have their folk message for the magical gardener. If the first one seen in summertime is white then prosperity lies ahead for the entire year, but should it be brown, times are likely to be hard. Oddly enough, the Scots were at one time convinced that butterflies with red wings were witches in disguise.

Most insects have their part to play in your magical garden. A black snail which crosses your garden path indicates rainfall. To see a spider in the evening is a good omen, but if seen in the morning there is trouble in store. It is unlucky to kill a black beetle, the penalty for so doing being an unwanted shower of rain. Should you happen to live in the Isle of Man seven continuous wet days can be expected.

It goes without saying that every magic garden should be equipped with its floral weather guides since these have been so bountifully supplied by nature. If the bramble blossoms early in the month of June one can anticipate an early harvest, just as the broom "having plenty of blossoms is the sign of a fruitful year", according to proverbial gardening lore. And again: "When the hawthorne bloom too early shows/We shall have too many snows."

For those with the determination to exercise positive control over the weather there is an old superstition that cutting or burning fern brings a shower of rain. The fern is also good for a number of other magical purposes including curing the stomach ache and the toothache. The house leek, often known as the syngreen by country folk, supplies magical protection to buildings and should of course be allowed to grow on house and outhouse roofs to provide a supernatural safeguard against fire and lightning. Its sap is credited with the power to relieve burns.

Now for a few psychic hints for those who insist that no garden is complete without its vegetable patch.

A potato kept in the pocket is an antidote for rheumatism, but only if it has been begged or stolen. The first crop of new potatoes must be eaten by the whole family or the remainder of the crop will rot.

All vegetables must be planted in a north–south orientation if they are to prosper.

Beans were at one time the true embodiments of magic; there is a strong belief in the north of England that kidney beans must be planted on May 3rd if the crop is to prosper. Lovelorn maids can lure laggardly lovers by the simple process of arranging seven beans in a circle and burying them under the turf where the young man is expected to tread. Once he places his feet on the spot he is irretrievably lost.

It is supposed to be unlucky for a woman to plant a large number of lettuces in her garden; if she is single she will never marry, and if married she will never have children.

In order to attract money into purse or pocket you must plant mint in your garden or carry it as a lucky charm.

As we mentioned earlier, parsley is a most ominous plant. By transplanting it you make a free gift of your vegetable garden to Satan, while to give a bunch away results in bad luck.

Onions would appear at first sight to be unlikely candidates for romance, yet these humble vegetables have played an important part in love magic. If a girl places an onion under her pillow on St Thomas' Eve she will dream of her future husband. Alternatively, to discover his name she must scratch the initial of each of the men she fancies on a separate onion with a pin and place them in the corner of a cupboard. The onion marked with the initials of the husband-to-be will be the first to sprout.

In conclusion, the garden must be walled because only within a formal enclosure can there exist the serenity which makes successful magical gardening possible. There should of course be a presiding genius, say a stone gnome, to cast his aura of magic over all. But better still would be a magical gardener with "green fingers" to supply that necessary supernatural touch to the seasonal round of delving, planting and harvesting within that realm, so carefully insulated from the world outside the garden gate.

CHAPTER TEN

Flower Festivals

As far back as one can venture into history the flower festival has been an established social institution, one of the earliest examples being the Floralia celebrated in Italy in honour of the Goddess of Flowers. These old customs largely disappeared with the advent of Christianity, but in the Middle Ages floral games were held at Toulouse and Barcelona. However, in the days of the troubadours the ceremonies were brought to the highest degree of perfection. Those minstrels of courtly love and poets of Languedoc competed for a golden violet, the prize awarded for the best poem submitted to a panel of judges and read before a vast multitude of poetry lovers. The troubadours, together with their romantic effusions, were suppressed when the Papacy decided to destroy the civilization and heresies of Languedoc.

In the year 1355 three prizes were awarded, a golden violet for the winning song, a Spanish jasmine for the best pastorale and a yellow acacia for the finest ballad.

In 1540 the wealthy poetess Clemence Isaura left the bulk of her fortune to be spent on prizes in a floral contest, the fête to be held on the first three days of May, the traditional time of the Floralia of earlier ages. The ceremonies commenced with the strewing of Isaura's tomb with roses; this was followed by a sermon and the giving of alms. Despite the hostility to pagan survivals expressed by the Church, the rites survived until the French Revolution and were then revived in the year 1806.

Salency in France was the scene of a romantic contest in which a crown of roses was awarded to the girl who had been acclaimed "the most amiable, modest and dutiful". The founder of the festival, St Medard, Bishop of Noyon, had the honour of awarding his own sister the floral crown and she became, therefore, the first "Rosière de Salency".

During the Middle Ages a curious Battle of Flowers took place at Treviso in northern Italy. A mock castle was built in the heart of the city, and was defended by a garrison of girls against a besieging army of ardent youths. For missiles the contestants used roses, lilies and narcissi and cascades of rose-water. Visitors from many lands attended the spectacle, including the Emperor Frederick Barbarossa who found it "a most pleasing diversion". The sexual connotations in this floral game are self-evident as are its links with the Mayday rites of peasant Europe.

It is interesting to observe in the celebrations of the Middle Ages features belonging to the earlier pagan civilizations. Like the Romans, the medieval nobles reserved the most beautiful flowers for their festive rites.

The Reverend T.F. Thistleton-Dyer reminds readers of his *Folk-lore of Plants* of the continuity between the floral rites of the ancients and those of later times when he says: "Indeed many of the flowers in request nowadays for ceremonial use in our own and other countries may be traced back to this period; the symbolical meaning attached to certain plants having survived after a lapse of many centuries."

The use of flowers in the British coronation ceremony is discussed in that curious compendium of royal rituals *Old Court Customs* by the Hon. Mrs Armytage. In her description of the coronation procession of King George IV we are told that: "Miss Fellowes and her maids, strewing the choicest blossoms as they headed the long procession, have of course not been included in the shortened ceremonies of later reigns and the description of the dresses worn by the ladies comes from official records. Miss Fellowes wore a dress of white satin, which in the present day would appear very scanty in width, length or trimming; a mantle of scarlet cloth lined with satin hung from the shoulders, while gold wheat ears, grapes and laurel leaves were mixed in a wreath for the head.

"The attendant flower maids wore white crêpe dresses over white satin, with large garlands of flowers from the shoulder across the dress to the edge of the skirt, chaplets of flowers in the hair; and large baskets of the choicest blossoms were carried between each couple of these young ladies who had been chosen for this honourable duty. Thus was the splendid ceremonial of the coronation."

To the great majority of people the word carnival conjures up scenes of wild abandon, of fantastically garbed men, women, girls and boys, escorting giants and man-made monsters through the streets of a southern city, garlanded with flowers and lost to everything but their own pleasures. In its original form a carnival was a sensational event, an extravagant and often licentious farewell to the pleasures of the flesh held on the eve of Lent – that period of enforced abstention. The word carnival is believed to be based on Carne-Vale, or alternatively *Carnis levare*, the farewell to meat from the diet. In Britain a surviving relic of this tradition is the frivolous Shrove Tuesday pancake ceremony in which pancakes are tossed into the air before being eaten. The pancake ritual was based originally upon the need to consume all the fat and eggs in the home – a gluttonous orgy before the dietary prohibitions of Lent.

At no time in this country during the Christian era does there appear to have been a festival which even remotely resembled the carnivals of the Continent which have been well described as a "combination of circus parade and a native war dance". However, as the folklore writer Sabine Baring Gould observed long ago, the modern European ceremony is infinitely more respectable than the rites upon which it was based, the Floralia of classical times. Even the Battle of Flowers appears to have been introduced into the Mediterranean area by orgiastically-minded Greek settlers. Modern flower lovers have on more than one occasion expressed their grief at the ruthless sacrifice of flowers in a gladiatorial arena of synthetic ecstasy. Sir Frederick Treves once described the carnival at Cannes thus: "The humble village feast has become a means of making money and an opportunity for clamour, licence and display."

On the Riviera, which was once Italian as far as Nice, the floral frolics are at their most riotous, with roses, violets, carnations and showers of confetti employed as missiles by the participants. Yet the French seem to observe the floral games with infinitely greater decorum than the Italians and their more sober style is reflected in the *mardi gras* of New Orleans, which long remained a

Gallic cultural enclave.

In the Channel Isles, the island of Jersey has its own floriana which was first introduced during the celebrations accompanying the coronation of King Edward VII and Queen Alexandra in 1902. It is said that the Jersey celebrations have become the greatest floral carnival in Europe, although they are in no way connected with the Lenten rites as are the celebrations elsewhere. One of the highlights of the day is their procession, which attracts many thousands of visitors and features exotic floats including a lifesize floral elephant and a floral windmill.

Episodes of the island's history are commemorated florally on this day, including the famous Battle of Jersey of 1781 in which the island militia and the English garrison successfully withstood an attack by the French fleet. The hero of that occasion, Major Francis Pearson, lies buried in the town church.

After the floral process a Battle of Flowers takes place with the usual cascades of blossoms hurled at everyone in sight. However, great care is taken by the safety-conscious organizers to ensure that all the "weapons" have been previously stripped of wires or thorns. This modern version of the ancient Battle of Flowers combines elements of the Lenten festival with that of May Day, since there is a special Jersey Queen who rides in a coach beautifully garlanded with scented flowers. It is also reminiscent of the ancient procession of the Corybantes in which the goddess Cybele was pelted with white roses. So successful was this expression of popular joy that the Battle of Flowers has been repeated annually ever since on the Thursday prior to the August Bank Holiday.

It seems that the same type of festival was once (and perhaps still is) celebrated in Iran during the season of the roses when the young men of the villages serenaded the public with song and at the same time assailing everyone they met with roses, receiving in return gifts of coins from passers-by.

The Battle of Flowers is living history. One is reminded of the splendid processions of Rome, when following a military success, the victorious commander staged a triumphant march through the streets of the capital amidst cascades of falling flowers which were thrown from the windows and roofs of the houses along the route.

Yet another relic of ancient times is well-dressing which is almost certainly a survival of the *Fontinalia* of ancient Rome when the citizens garlanded their fountains and wells with flowers. The modern well-dressing ceremony, which takes place on Ascension Day, involves the decoration of the wells with flowers and the boughs of trees in a ritual which has survived almost unscathed from pre-Reformation times.

At Tissington in Derbyshire where the rite is known as "well-flowering", five wells are dressed in the most beautiful fashion with flowers set in clay and placed upon boards. They are surrounded with branches of laurel and whitethorn and so arranged as to suggest the most intricately designed mosaic work.

Young people often cast flowers into wells to discover from the way they fall whether or not their love affair is likely to be successful. A recent visit by the author to the famous well at St David's Head in Pembrokeshire revealed the presence of numerous flowers in the water, including purple lilac accompanied by coins cast there by superstitious visitors. Prior to the Reformation it was customary for villagers who lived in the Celtic areas of the British Isles to make pilgrimages to wells and springs and offer flowers to the saints and martyrs to whom the wells had been dedicated.

Rivers were sometimes "sprinkled with flowers" for the same reason, as we read in Dryden's "The Fleece":

> . . . o'er the dimpled stream a thousand flowers
> Pale lilies, roses, violets and pinks
> Mixed with the greens of burnet, mint and thyme.

The connections between floral art and that of the dance are world-wide and of ancient lineage. Among the Greeks, for example, there was a fascinating mimetic dance representing the nuptial rites of Bacchus and Ariadne, and a flower dance in which the performers sang of roses, violets and parsley, that ancient symbol of death:

> Oh where are my roses, Oh where are my violets
> and where is my beautiful parsley?
> Are these then my roses? Are these then my violets?
> And is this my beautiful parsley?

In Greek antiquity parsley was the prize awarded at the Nemean Games.

One of the more striking features of the Japanese New Year celebrations is the wealth of floral decoration which accompanies it. Standing sentinel at every household door at this time are two plants representing the male and female principles in nature. On the left is *Pinus densiflora* which symbolizes the female, and on the right is the *Pinus thumbergius*, symbolizing the male. The pine represents the idea of durability which has withstood the ravages of time. A rope which is suspended from the branches of the Melei Japonica to keep evil spirits at bay is entwined around a scarlet lobster, the symbol of old age. Among other symbols of Japanese good luck and long life are ferns, seaweed, chestnuts and the dried fruit of the kaki.

The Japanese are famous for their flower festivals which number five in all: the Go Sekku, celebrated on the seventh day of the New Year and known as the Fête of the Seven Grasses; the Festival of Dolls, celebrated on the third day of the third month and held in honour of girls, is the occasion for lavish displays of cherry and peach blossom; the Festival of Boys, held on the fifth day of the fifth month, is celebrated with the early chrysanthemum, the iris and the moso-chiku, a bamboo-like plant. The fourth fête, the Tanabata, is held on the seventh day of the seventh month which is one of the more auspicious days of the Japanese year. In this case the chosen decorations are the bamboo combined with paper chrysanthemums of seven different colours. One real flower must be included in the display if good luck is to be maintained. On the ninth day of the ninth month comes the Chrysanthemum Fête, a festival of Chinese origin in which chrysanthemums of five different colours predominate: white, light red, dark red, blue or purple, and yellow, each flower having its individual symbolism. In Japan the chrysanthemum is the flower of Autumn and the emblem of the Mikado.

A "returning flower", in other words one which blooms twice in the same year, is displayed at farewell parties to indicate good wishes and hopes for a safe return for the traveller. The same principle is observed at special assemblies which are held immediately before a battle or other unpredictable event.

In Japan, where a bride is given the name flower-daughter by her husband's family, all noblewomen were called flower maidens. The Japanese are deeply steeped in flower symbolism. All the flower colours have important meanings, while flowers in general symbolize the search for truth. Floral arrangement is a mystical rite which confers upon the arranger special virtues, powers and qualities, as below:

Name of Arrangement	*Quality*
Chobo furyu	Gentleness
Dokuraku katarazu	Light-heartedness in solitude
Mui-tanen	Serenity in face of sorrow
Sawaku ribetsu	Self-control and self-denial
Seikon gyojo	Mental and bodily health
Shimbutsku haizo	Religious fervour
Shujin meichi	Respect for one's fellows
Somolco meichi	Kinship with plants and trees

There are five lineal arrangements to represent the five elements and the five virtues, while the hanging-boat arrangement indicates a voyage. The natural arrangement is usually reserved for tea-rooms, for in Japan the tea-room is itself a symbolic centre, representing an oasis in the desert wastes where the exhausted travellers may find renewal and repose.

Readers will not need to be reminded of the wide range of activities in our national cavalcade of social and folk customs which involve the employment of flowers. From New Year in to Old Year out the seasons are bejewelled with curious, often ancient, and invariably interesting ceremonies in which flowers and plants have a symbolic role quite apart from their natural function which is to delight the eye and give pleasure to observers and participants alike. The floral folk calendar which follows makes no claim to comprehensiveness and is limited to the portrayal of the better known occasions which demonstrate in one way or another the survival of ancient flower and plant magic into modern times.

January 6th: Holy Thorn of Glastonbury. One of the floral miracles of the New Year is the flowering of the Holy Thorn of Glastonbury in Somerset at midnight. The present tree, a hawthorn, has been grown from a cutting from the fabulous Holy Thorn planted by St Joseph of Arimathea. St Joseph is said to have planted his hawthorn staff in the earth where it took root and flowered, and the miracle was regarded by the saint as a sign that a church must be

Glastonbury Thorn

set up on the site. Each year a sprig from the tree is sent to the sovereign.

January 6th: The Haxey Hood Contest. Commencing with the New Year there is an ancient ritual called the Haxey Hood Contest which takes place at Haxey in Lincolnshire each January 6th, Old Christmas Day, this being the day on which Christmas was celebrated prior to the calendar changes introduced in 1752. In this contest teams known as Boggans struggle to obtain possession of a leather hood about 2 feet 6 inches long and 3 inches wide, the prizes consisting of free drinks in any of the local pubs. Originally the contestants wore scarlet jerkins and velvet caps. Today they wear tall hats decorated with flowers.

January 30th: Honouring the Martyr King. King Charles I, the Martyr, was beheaded by the English Republicans in 1649. He receives due honour each January 30th, the anniversary of his execution, when the base of his statue is decorated with wreaths and similar floral tributes, a custom introduced in 1892. When the statue was removed for safe-keeping elsewhere during World War II, the plinth continued to be decorated with floral wreaths by those who honoured Charles' memory.

March 3rd: St Mary's, Scilly Isles. St Mary's, the largest of the Scilly Isles, lies off the coast of Cornwall near Land's End. The island holds three annual flower shows, the first in January, the second in early March and the third at Easter. Visitors from all over Europe are present at these shows, which are organized by the Isles of Scilly Horticultural Society. These islands are world-famous for their mild climate which makes possible a wealth of luxurious vegetation, early flowers and spring vegetables.

April: Battersea Easter Parade. With the advance of Spring, Battersea Park in London celebrates the awakening of the floral year with its own Easter Parade which is held in the park. The Battersea equivalent of the May Queen is the Easter Princess, and there is also a parade of floats lavishly decorated with flowers.

April 18th: Royal Maundy Celebration. This is observed on Maundy Thursday and is based on the ancient rite of washing the feet of the poor in memory of Christ's ablution of the Apostles. Today money is distributed instead, but those participating in the ceremony carry posies of flowers, a custom which dates to the time when the feet of beggars were purified with herbs before being washed by the monarch.

April: Southend Flower Festival. One of the most inspiring of the modern Spring rites is the annual Flower Festival held at Southend on Sea on the Thames estuary during the last week of April. The highlight of the ceremony is an immense display of bulbs and plants which make the occasion one of the most famous and interesting in the British Isles. Southend also holds a carnival procession in August which is famed for its elaborately decorated floral floats.

April: Hungerford Hocktide Ceremony. At the end of April the festival of Hocktide is celebrated at Hungerford, Berkshire, with peculiarly local features. Two tithing men, or tuttymen, toss oranges to children as they parade through the town carrying staffs ornamented with wild flowers. The custom is thought to have originated in the fourteenth century. ("Tutty", a word from the west of England, means flowers or nosegays.) It is an occasion enjoyed by all, and few of the tuttymen return to their homes at the conclusion of the celebrations as soberly as when they left them.

April: Birmingham Spring Festival. This festival of modern vintage has been held at Birmingham during the last week of April since 1960, when it was inaugurated to commemorate the fourth centenary of the introduction of tulips into Europe. The presence of large numbers of visitors from the European mainland, particularly from Holland, has given this particular flower festival a truly international status.

May Day Festival. The old-time May Day festival with its May King and rustic jollifications is no more; only its pale shadow is discernible in our modern merrymaking on May 1st. In Rutland up to a generation or so ago children gave their parents garlands of flowers picked on May Eve. In Horncastle, Lincolnshire, which was once the site of a Roman temple, boys marched in procession daffodil and the acanthus."

During the late Middle Ages the gardens of the great nobles appear to have been pitifully small and considered of little importance, even until the beginning of the sixteenth century. The immensely powerful Earl of Northumberland, whose establishment consisted of no less than one hundred and fifty persons, employed only one gardener who was paid by the hour. However, by the close of the next century the formal Tudor garden had become popular; this was succeeded by the fashionable Dutch garden, which remained in vogue until the eighteen seventies. By the middle of the seventeenth century, the garden had become a poetic vision, hence Abraham Cowley's:

> My garden painted o'er
> With nature's hand, not art's, and pleasures yield
> Horace might envy in his Sabine field.

During the eighteenth century the gardens of the nobility were gradually cleared of their "tonsured greens" and later under the influence of Capability Brown (1715–1783), returned to picturesque waste, the wild grasses of the estate being permitted to advance right up to the walls of the house itself, a refreshing tribute to naturalism and the Rousseauan concept of the noble savage.

John Timbs, in his *Popular Errors* published in 1856, says of nineteenth-century English gardens: "One great error into which we have fallen in England is that nearly all our gardens, such as they are, are alike. The small walled-in garden of the villas in the neighbourhood of London; the distribution of shrubs and flowerbeds of the London squares; the college gardens of Oxford and Cambridge; the pleasure gardens of our country residences, both great and small, from those of Buckingham Palace and St James's Park to the humblest parsonage; are on precisely the same model. They may be said, one and all to be formed on a plan of which the gardens of the Petit Trianon of Versailles are an admirable caricature."

In justice to their pioneering work we now pay tribute to those intrepid explorers and dedicated botanists to whom we are indebted for the study and introduction of so many foreign flowers, plants and trees over the centuries. We begin with Theophrastus of Lesbos, a Greek of the fourth century B.C., who published several treatises including an "Enquiry into Plants", one of the oldest surviving botanical works. It was Theophrastus who carried out a survey of the flora of the Mediterranean region and studied the then unknown tropical flowers of the Middle East and India. Pliny the Elder, who lived in the first century B.C., wrote a Natural History – one of the earliest studies of the realm of nature.

His contemporary, the Greek Dioscorides who lived in the first century A.D., produced a work on herbs which served as a medical guide for over fourteen hundred years, and was described as one of the most valuable botanical studies ever written. It has been translated into every language from Anglo-Saxon to Persian. The Anglo-Saxon period witnessed a revival of botanical lore accompanied by leech books and herbals based largely upon fragmentary traditions inherited from the Greek and Roman civilization.

A number of Greek herbals written on papyrus had survived the holocaust of the religious revolution which brought Christianity to the fore and trampled classical learning into the dust, but each had been successively rendered less intelligible as it was copied and re-copied by slavish clerks who had no understanding of the works they transcribed.

From ancient Egypt comes the earliest known picture of a plant; it is carved on pieces of slate and represents a palm. The figure covers two fragments which are housed at the Ashmolean Museum at Oxford and the British Museum, respectively. There is, however, an earlier representation of a branch with leaves on a piece of reindeer horn found at Arcy-sur-Cure in France. As in other palaeolithic drawings this plant is unidentifiable.

Around 1500 B.C. Thotmes III dispatched an expedition to Syria which returned to Egypt with many hitherto unknown plants. These were depicted on the walls of Karnack accompanied by the following inscription: "Year 25 of the King of Upper Egypt and Lower Egypt, Living for Ever. Plants which his Majesty found in the country of Syria. All plants that grow, all goodly flowers that are in the Divine land."

For early writings containing illustrations of flowers and other plants one should refer to the *Book of Hours* to which the medieval illuminators devoted their finest art. A copy in the National Library of Paris contains pictures of scores of plants most interestingly portrayed, the work of Jean de Bourdichon, one of the great illuminators.

It was not until the ninth century that the first literary approach to gardening manifested itself in Christian Europe; it took poetic form in the writings of Walafred Strabo, a monk of Lake Constance who produced a *Hortulus* (Little Garden) consisting of twenty-seven poems each of which concentrated upon an individual plant. A nature lover, Strabo was never happier than in the Spring "when herbs and flowers were stirred by the west wind". In the fourteenth century Bartholomeus Anglicus, an English friar, published his *De Proprietatbius Rerum* – an encyclopaedia one volume of which was devoted to herbs and trees.

John Gardner, a fifteenth-century writer of whom practically nothing else is known, was responsible for the earliest horticultural treatise in the English tongue, *Feate of Gardening* published in 1440, which consisted entirely of verse. Not until the Renaissance with the rediscovery of ancient learning did the long-forgotten works of the classical botanists find their way into Europe and lead ultimately to the modern scientific study of plants.

The deluge of botanical lore now in full spate coincided with the introduction of many strange and exotic plants from newly-discovered America. Now the cobwebs of the past were blowing away; a revolution in scholarship was in progress, and seemed irresistible.

In the sixteenth century William Turner, famous as "The Father of British Botany", identified and classified no less than 238 English plants. Among other pioneers of botany during the same period was John Gerard, whose famous sixteenth-century *Herball or Historie of Plants* was in fact pirated from Dodoen's *Temptades* (1583). Gerard was responsible for a valuable study of the flowers which grew in his own garden.

From the seventeenth century onwards, gardening began to exist as a sphere of activity in its own right, for it was at last severed from the cultivation of herbs for utilitarian purposes. Plants and flowers began to be valued for their beauty; aestheticism had come of age. It was John Parkinson (1567–1650) who produced the earliest illustrated book on ornamental plants, using a highly individual system of classification which involved designating flowers which failed to fit in with his theory as "the unknown tribe". Parkinson has earned the gratitude of subsequent generations for his deep interest in gardens and wild flowers.

John Tradescant (the elder), who became royal gardener to King Charles I, was a dedicated collector of new plants from abroad. He had as his contemporary Nicholas Culpeper, the famous herbalist/astrologer who, like others of his generation, believed that each plant lay under the jurisdiction of a particular planet, a theme he discussed at length in his book *The English Physician Enlarged*, published in 1653. Culpeper was deeply involved with the occult and set up as a healing wizard in seventeenth-century London, on one occasion being compelled to defend his activities before a court of law.

However, it was John Evelyn, the diarist and one of the founders of the Royal Society, who brought about the true arboreal and horticultural revolution, having become acquainted with the art of gardening during his extensive travels on the Continent. His *magnum opus, Sylva, or a Discourse of Forest Trees* which he published in 1664, was responsible for popularizing the establishment of plantations on the great estates of the nobility.

Sayes Court in Deptford came to Evelyn as an inheritance by right of his wife and here he spent a happy life dedicated to tree planting and gardening. In 1690 he came into possession of Wotton, his family seat, and there took up residence. Sayes Court was let to a series of temporary tenants one of whom was Peter the Great; this barbaric Russian Tsar left the garden in ruins, causing Evelyn intense anguish. A nineteenth-century writer has summed up Evelyn thus: "He taught the rural aristocracy a duty they owed to themselves and their country: and since his time they have well performed it."

John Ray (1627–1705) was responsible for an invaluable gardening work, *Flora, Ceres and Pomona* which appeared in 1665. In it he discussed "French Flowers", annuals and biennials as well as fruits of all kinds. The Reverend Samuel Gilbert, who became Ray's son-in-law and in due course took over his nursery, produced his own book *A Florist's Vade Mecum* in 1683, which formed a useful guide to the gardener's year despite much of it having been written in verse.

The greatest Continental botanist of the seventeenth century was unquestionably J. Pitton de Tournefort, who died in 1708 after a lifetime dedicated to the study of plants. He was responsible for inventing a system of botanical classifications which remained predominant until Linnaeus appeared on the scene in the eighteenth century.

However, we now enter the Age of Enlightenment in which gardening was transformed into an art form. The introduction of new plants from Africa in addition to those from America was in full flood, and it became usual for botanists to accompany the ships which were beginning to explore the outermost limits of the earth, opening the world's eyes as well as its markets to plants and flowers hitherto undreamed of. To this era belongs George London (died 1717), the famous superintendent of the Royal Gardens in the reign of William III, who with Henry Wise laid out the gardens at Blenheim Palace, and in addition constructed Hampton Court maze. Others of this period were Thomas Fairchild (1667–1729), author of *The City Gardener* which discussed flowers useful to Londoners; and Philip Miller (1692–1771), known as "The Prince of Gardeners" and author of the famous *Gardeners' Dictionary* published in 1731.

Gardening, botany and horticulture can be said to have reached maturity, in the scientific sense, with the advent of Carl von Linnaeus (1707–1778), the Swedish botanist whose sexual system of plant classification and binomial system of nomenclature placed botany once and for all upon a secure scientific foundation. Linnaeus' contribution produced order out of the chaos of the earlier theorists, assembling the writings and ideas to form a true synthesis. According to Alice M. Coates' *Flowers and Their Histories*, he was responsible for naming "more flowers than Eve". Linnaeus was a true man of parts, a scientist of wide and varied attainments, an expert in zoology, entomology and mineralogy and a brilliant physician. His logical mind substituted for the vague assumptions of the past a system of terse and clear diagnosis which found acceptance among scientific thinkers.

And now we have arrived at the nineteenth century which witnessed the advent of the gardening journals, reflecting the growing interest felt by the middle classes in the new status symbols – gardens and flowers. Among these were Curtis' *Botanical Magazine, The Botanical Repository, The Botanical Garden*, and similar publications which not only found a ready market but widened the interest in what had hitherto been an aristocratic pursuit.

A new type of book also appeared on the scene with Henry Phillips' *Flora Historica* published in 1824, Elizabeth Kent's *Flora Domestica*, John Claudius Loudon's *Encyclopedia of Gardening* and his *Encyclopedia of Plants* and *The English Flower Garden* published by William Robinson in 1883 which became essential reading for every serious-minded cultivator of plants and flowers. A later work, *The English Rock Garden* published by Reginald Farrar in 1922 remains a classic among gardening literature to this day.

It was one of the truly enjoyable functions of democracy and an interesting aspect of the advance of leisure, that all social ranks could now enjoy a recreation which had originally been confined to the very few. However, it will be accepted that the art has never been plebeianized; every gardener is a creative artist and a lover of beauty and is automatically enlisted into the ranks of the true aristocracy of nature.

Gardening and plant lore have profoundly influenced our thinking, and have made a great impact upon our language and, more particularly, the phrases we use. For example: the *seeds of love* may turn into *a budding romance* and blossom into *a family tree.* Kent is known as the Garden of England in popular usage because of its fertility, and the same is said of Worcestershire. Carlow in Ireland is the Garden of Erin; Touraine is the Garden of France; Andalusia the Garden and Granary of Spain; Tucuman is the Garden of Argentina; Colorado Springs in the United States the Garden of the Gods; while the Garden of the World is the vast area of fertile land in the Mississippi area. Kansas is known far and wide as the Garden of the West. The East Indian Malayan Archipelago is the Garden of the East. There are also Devil's Gardens and Devil's Acres in England, in other words patches of wasteland given over to thistles – which were once and probably still are weeds of Satan, the inveterate foe of Adam, our first gardener. The Garden Sect was the name of a school of philosophy founded by Epicurus in 306 B.C. which met in an Athenian garden.

Now we turn to the history and mystery of the edible plants which in countries other than the British Isles are almost invariably given greater prominence than flowers.

Endless are the contributions which plant life has made to the well-being of humanity in the realms of medicine and food; sadly we have to consider that the cruel slave trade was one of the vehicles of the migration, of plants from Africa to America for the slave owners were determined to feed their captives as cheaply as possible.

The basic story of agriculture has to be told if the lore of the garden is to be fully explored. As is well known, the civilizations of antiquity were developed by grain-growing populations; in Asia it was the Chinese, Indians and Japanese, in the Near East the Babylonians, Israelites and Syrians among others, and in Europe the Romans and Greeks. The Maya and Aztec civilizations of the Americas were cultivators of cereals.

Barley, one of the first of the grains grown by man, has been cultivated from prehistoric times onwards. Incidentally, the Hindus utilized barley grain in religious rites, especially at weddings possibly because, as in China, the seed symbolized masculine virility. Today only the most impoverished peoples eat barley bread, and its use is mainly confined to brewing.

The United States' passion for buckwheat griddle cakes could never have been satisfied had not the seed been brought to Europe in the first place by the returning Crusaders. In France it still bears the name of Saracen corn. Maize or Indian corn, a plant once exclusive to the Americas where it has been cultivated for some three thousand years, was regarded by the Aztecs with veneration. They had their God of Maize and regarded it sacrilegious even to tread on the grains where they lay on the earth. There is an American Indian legend which says that the first maize was brought to mankind in the beak of a crow and consequently no crow is ever prevented from feasting on the growing crop. From the time of Columbus maize has remained one of the most important of all European crops, being used not only as food but as an ingredient of beer which is brewed from the fermented grain.

The pearly seeds of the millet, the smallest of all the cereals, were among the crops cultivated by the ancient Assyrians, and it is to Herodotus that we are indebted for the earliest information about this plant which he saw during his travels in the Near East during the fifth century B.C. Millet is now extensively cultivated the world over, and in the United States is an invaluable cattle feed.

The Lotus-Eaters

Oats, like millet, have been grown from time immemorial, and provided food for horses in Central Asia as early as 2000 B.C. The development of oat cultivation is closely connected with a horse economy and it became a staple crop following the introduction of this animal into a community. Once oats had become acclimatized to the cold regions of Northern Europe they soon became one of the basic foods, as in the case of the British Isles where they arrived with the invading Roman cavalry.

It is said that the art of rice cultivation was taught to the Chinese by their Emperor Shun Nung who lived between 2800 and 2700 B.C. This important event was commemorated for over 4,500 years by a ceremony performed annually on February 5th. On this day the Emperor, accompanied by his principal ministers and officials, made a ceremonial furrow in the earth with a plough to inaugurate the tilling season. Afterwards the people gathered clumps of the newly-dug earth and scattered them around their own paddy, as a magical charm to guarantee them a bountiful crop. So important is rice to the people of China that one of their traditional greetings on meeting a neighbour is to enquire, "Have you eaten your rice today?" Rice is so important a magical symbol that accidentally knocking over a rice bowl at the table is considered an omen of misfortune, while showering a newly-wed couple with rice grains is a fertility charm to ensure they have a large and happy family. In the West this custom has long been superseded by throwing confetti over the bride and bridegroom outside the church.

Rye, which is a native of Western Asia and the Middle East, is not only the hardiest of all the cereal grasses but has the additional advantage of being able to grow in extremely poor soil. It is therefore one of the "poverty" foods which in Europe was milled into dark flour and made into black bread. However, in Canada and the United States rye is used for the distillation of malt liquors. The German peasants once believed that the rye fields were the haunts of a fertility spirit known as the "Rye Wolf" or "roggen wolf", and it was usual for the last sheaf of the crop to be left untouched by the harvesters to provide shelter for the creature until the following spring. Whether demon or fertility spirit, this monster had much in common with the spirit of the wheatfields of Western Europe. Wheat, the oldest of all the grain cereals cultivated by mankind, was known in the Stone Age, the

Neolithic Age, and in the Ancient World where it was worshipped as a god. The Hittites had a harvest goddess called Ibritz, the Egyptians their Nepri, the Greeks Demeter, and the Romans Ceres, daughter of the god Saturn. Her hair was the colour of corn and she was honoured at two ceremonies: the Cerealana, and a lesser festival, the Ambarvalia.

A curious ritual known as "Crying the Neck", once an essential part of the wheat or corn harvest ceremony, was described by Robert Hunt, a collector of Devonshire and Cornish folklore in the early years of the nineteenth century: "After the wheat is all cut on most farms in Cornwall and Devon, the harvest people have a custom of 'crying the neck' . . . an old man or someone well qualified with the ceremonies used on the occasion when the labourers are reaching the last field of wheat, goes round to the shocks of sheaves and picks out a little bundle of all the best ears he can find: this bundle he ties up very neat and trim, and plaits and arranges with straws very tastefully. This is called the 'neck' of wheat. . . . After this the harvesters stand in a circle and all begin to cry out 'The neck' raising their hats above their heads. After three such cries they chant 'We Yen! We Yen! We Yen!' Then there is a rush towards the farmhouse in pursuit of 'the neck' which is carried by one of the group. . . . The neck is hung in the farmhouse for as long as three or four harvests." Folklorists believe that in the original ceremony the person carrying the neck would have been sacrificed to the corn spirit.

The same reverence for the standing corn was extended to bread itself, this being the main article of diet in all corn-growing lands. Like the neck or corn dolly, bread was regarded as the embodiment of the corn spirit and treated with respect. It is still considered unlucky to throw bread away and even more so to burn it. In Roman Catholic countries such outrageous behaviour is said to "Make Our Lady Cry". Sometimes a cross is made on the dough before it is placed in the oven, this being the genesis of the Easter hot cross bun. Hot cross buns are sometimes preserved for years on end to bring good fortune to the house, while bread baked on Christmas Day is expected to protect the home against sickness.

It was always believed that spirit forces dominated cultivation, and it was necessary to propitiate them with magical rituals of one kind or another. These concepts lingered on until fairly recently, when they dissolved with considerable rapidity under the impact of scientific ideas.

The present century, however, has witnessed a gradual revival of superstitions of all kinds among flower lovers, even to the extent of planning a garden on supernatural principles, as laid down by the magicians of old.

CHAPTER NINE

The Magic Garden

For those with a superstitious attitude to horticulture, or perhaps more truthfully a lingering belief in magic, the idea of a garden deliberately designed to attract favourable psychic forces on the one hand and resistance to the encroachments of evil spirits on the other, offers an attractive prospect. The idea is by no means a novelty and belongs to an almost forgotten philosophy of life which decreed that certain fixed principles of harmony have to be observed in every aspect of existence including the house and garden.

What is sometimes called "landscape symbolism" is in reality a recognition of the divine in nature which should be respected whenever mankind trespasses upon her domain. The desert or wilderness provides one type of symbolism described as "the vast eternity of emptiness", although the artist will be aware that wandering in the wastelands can be a liberating experience, for these mental images are projected outwardly upon the skies and thus acquire much deeper meaning and enhanced vitality. From the desert one turns to the forest where the opposite rule applies, for here the environment presses upon the wanderer among the trees, imposing its will upon his consciousness; shaping his dreams; speaking his thoughts.

However, a formal garden symbolizes an enclosure and a separateness from the wilderness of nature, a place of escape and at the same time a sanctuary where man can apply his own concepts to the things that he grows.

Kenneth Clark is on record as defining a garden as "a flowery meadow cut off from the world'', a place where ''love human and divine could find fulfilment''. This could well have been the description of the Garden of Eden, but the idyllic concept is shared by imaginative gardeners everywhere.

The garden has also been described as a walled city and a symbol of the feminine in nature . . . a specially devised womb for the conception and growth of certain living forces. Some might say that it contains the secret of life itself. The gardens of ancient times, as portrayed in religious art, were sacred enclosures with feminine aspects as we read in the Song of Solomon: ''A garden locked is my sister, my bride, a garden locked is a fountain sealed.''

Some psychologists regard the garden as a symbol of the unconscious mind, a sanctified enclosure, while the menacing forest is seen as the primordial instinct struggling to overcome man's efforts to control his destiny.

''In the garden all nature is subdued, ordered, selected and enclosed.'' Here in ancient times special plants and trees were planted to provide security against the intrusions of unharmonious elemental spirits, which threatened one's tranquillity.

Among the best known of protective trees is the apple which is a traditional luck-bringer, and an emblem of perpetual youth; also the rowan or mountain ash, which is believed to keep away witches and the evil eye; another is the almond which is a symbol of fruitfulness; while the medlar is a lucky fruit.

However, the underlying principle of the planning of a magic garden has first to be explained in detail.

In the first place it is vitally necessary to avoid plants and flowers which superstition over the ages has decreed must never be brought into the house. Among these is the first snowdrop of the year which derives its sinister reputation from the fact that it wears a ''shroud'' or old-fashioned burial robe and is an emblem of death. Then there is the daffodil, which ancient tradition associated with human sacrifice and for this reason a single bloom brings misfortune. Daffodils must be bunched before being brought inside, otherwise the shadow of sorrow will fall upon the occupants.

In planning the magic garden it is essential to render the earth ritually sterile; this involves clearing the ground of all previous plants, including flowers, herbs and weeds, although the purge should not be extended to trees which are luck-bringers. However, even the shape of a tree can render it an "undesirable" companion and for this reason "evil-looking" trees with ugly, menacing branches should be uprooted. It has to be remembered that plants are the abodes of spirits and that an adverse influence will be disseminated by an evil presence in whatever shape it assumes, and will possibly cast a blight upon the garden as a whole, as well as upon those who cultivate it.

Once the garden has been rendered spiritually sterile its architecture has to be carefully planned. A two-foot diameter circle representing the sacred heart must be laid out in the centre of the plot, the lines of the circle being indicated by stones, preferably white ones for purity. In one sense the circle may be seen as the emblem of the moon goddess although this symbolism also represents the solar eye, otherwise the sun, and is therefore based on the principle of eternal perfection. Some magical gardeners have a preference for a double circle since this represents the divine marriage between heaven and earth, and the sun and moon.

It is from the heart of the circle that one plans the entire series of operations which follow. The garden has to be planted in sections which radiate outwardly from the centre in imitation of the rays of the sun, and within these clearly defined areas the flowers and herbs are to be planted. However, each of the four corners of the garden must have its appointed protective tree: the apple, the rowan, the medlar and the mountain ash. The sector allocated to herbs must be restricted to plants with beneficent supernatural qualities and placed under the guardianship of a laurel and three lilies as a safeguard against poisonous influences as they affect herbs. The cultivation of flowers and plants has to be governed by strict observance of the sacred laws which have endowed each blossom with its specific property, hence the laurel, symbol of immortality, and the lily, the heraldic symbol of purity.

White flowers come under the jurisdiction of the moon and should therefore be planted so as to be visible throughout the four seasons, from January snowdrops, via spring hyacinths, summer white roses, and white chrysanthemums of autumn to the ever welcome Christmas rose. At one time it was believed that white flowers were inhabited by "moon spirits" who made their appearance at the full moon. The most favourable months

The Magic Garden

for seeing these coy elementals were July, August and September.

According to an article on the subject in the magazine *Prediction*, sprites materialize in a wide variety of shapes; those with trumpet-shaped crowns, for example, making their homes among trumpet-shaped petals. The author of this article, Madeline Montalban, advises her readers ". . . to offer up white flowers to the Goddess of the Moon on the night that the New Moon can be seen in the sky to bring in a fortunate month ahead."

There is a magic flower for all seasons as we shall find when we turn to the golden blossoms which are invariably dedicated to Apollo the sun god. All yellow flowers must be planted in the sunniest quarter of the garden and these include sunflowers, marigolds, and even yellow-tinted roses. Each of these serves to emphasize the cosmic relationship between your garden and the realm of nature with which you seek to establish harmony.

Then there must be a "planetary plot" which should incorporate a number of plants and flowers with important astrological attributes; these include the flowering shrubs. Beginning with Aries, otherwise the Lord of Mars, we find a role for the humble thistle which, as the symbol of vitality, should be planted not too far from the house, despite its traditional associations with the Devil. The thistle has a complex personality, for it is not only the symbol of austerity and rejection, being known as the Devil's grain, but at the same time is sacred to the warrior god Thor and the Virgin Mary, and in that sense should be considered a protective plant.

Among other plants belonging to the Aries group are those with peppery scents (such as *Clethra alfifolia*, the sweet pepper bush) and also the geranium which is a luck-bringer. There are, in fact, a number of geranium attributes to bear in mind when planting. Dark geraniums symbolize melancholy, "oak" geraniums friendship, the scarlet variety brings gaiety, while the rose variety represents the power of choice, and the silver ones memory.

So much for geraniums. Next come nasturtiums and flame red roses. The former is the symbol of patriotism, while the rose symbolizes fiery passion and can be expected to arouse the flames of

decorated with coronets, chains and cushions of flowers and bearing crosses of yew entwined with cuckoo pint and bluebells.

There exists an old tradition in the British Isles that the flowering hawthorn or may must never be brought indoors for fear of bad luck, but should instead be wreathed around the windows of the home on May morning. The order of wreathing had to be as follows: first the eastern side was decorated in honour of the sun; next the south in honour of mankind; the north was then wreathed to secure supernatural protection for the family, and finally the west side as a form of tribute to the Lord of Death.

The spirit of the season is now manifest in the large number of floral ceremonies which are held as long as the flowers bloom. In one of the more ancient survivals the May Queen of London is crowned on Hayes Common, Bromley, in a ritual which can trace its origins to the year 1516 when King Henry VIII participated in the merrymaking. The crown is placed on the lady's head by a girl dressed as a boy who has the role of Prince of Merrie England. Following the coronation all the minor May Queens of London pay homage to their new monarch.

Far more modern but none the less delightful is the Spalding, Lincolnshire, flower parade – or Tulip Festival – which was inaugurated in 1959 to celebrate the flowering of the tulips for which this area is famous. Along a four-mile route of fascinated onlookers parades a mile-long procession of tulip-decorated floats constructed with great ingenuity. Six million tulips are dedicated to this annual display which provides one of the most intriguing expressions of the carnival spirit in the British Isles.

May 8th: Furry Dance. The famous Furry Dance or Floral Dance performed annually at Helston, Cornwall, on what is known as Flora's Day is of unknown antiquity. The dancers carry garlands and wear sprigs of flowering hawthorn in their hats. This seems to suggest that there is a link between this West Country May Day festival and the ancient Floralia, the Roman festival of flowers. The Floral Song below is sung on this occasion:

Robin Hood and Little John
They both are gone to the fair.
And we'll go to the merry greenwood O.
And see what they do there O.

For we were up as soon as any day
For to fetch the summer home.
The summer and the May O
For the summer now has a-come O.

The day's events commence with the gathering of wild flowers and hawthorn branches early in the morning, which is completely in the tradition of the ancient English May Day rite.

May 21st: Lilies and Roses at the Tower. Each May 21st a ritual known as the Ceremony of the Lilies and Roses takes place in the Tower of London to commemorate the murder of the English King Henry VI in the Wakefield Tower on that day in 1471. Lilies and red roses are placed on the spot where he died by representatives of Eton College and King's College, Cambridge, both being establishments with which the King was associated. On the armorial bearings of Eton College are emblazoned three lilies, and on that of King's College three silver roses. It is customary for Eton lilies tied with a blue ribbon to be laid on the King's tomb (in St George's Chapel) on the same evening.

May 29th: Castleton Garland Day. The close of the month of merry-making sees the celebration of Garland Day at Castleton in Derbyshire where a procession led by a King and Queen rides through the town – the king with a beehive-shaped garland or haycock of flowers resting on his shoulders. At the parish church the garland is raised to the pinnacle of the tower where it remains for the next seven days. It seems to be generally agreed that this ceremony is the local version of the Oak Apple Day celebrations as May 29th was the birthday of Charles II. However, it has also been suggested that the celebration is much older, and associated with the Forest Court of John of Gaunt, Duke of Lancaster, who owned a great deal of land in this county.

End of May: Chelsea Flower Show. The Chelsea Flower Show, staged annually by the Royal Horticultural Society during the last week of May, is without doubt the greatest show of its kind in the world. As its central feature it has a gigantic marquee where a vast number of flowers are exhibited, including many new varieties. Also delighting the eye of the thousands who flock to

Chelsea at this time are flowering trees and shrubs of every imaginable type, together with displays of landscape gardening. The show has been held at Chelsea since 1913, having originally been established in Temple Gardens in 1888. The Chelsea Flower Show is not only internationally renowned, it is also one of the most attractive features of the London year.

The Royal Horticultural Society also holds floral displays in Westminster.

Flower shows appear to be of English origin, and can be dated to the seventeenth century when the gardeners of East Anglia held "florists' shows" to display tulips, auriculas and carnations. The idea spread to the Midlands and then to the country as a whole. Queen Adelaide, consort of William IV, became the first patron of the newly-created Metropolitan Society of Florists and Amateurs in 1832. Today the village flower show is one of the most firmly established folk festivals in the land.

May: Gawthorne May Festival. The annual Gawthorne May Feast which is held in Yorkshire around the first week of March was originally an integral part of the May Day celebration. The festival has as its focal point a very tall maypole set up in Gawthorne High Street, a custom first instituted in 1953, Coronation Year. Presiding over the ceremonies is a May Queen on horseback and there are numerous gaily decorated floats and tableaux passing through the town, all of them lavishly decorated with flowers and bunting.

June 23rd: Midsummer Anti-Witch Bonfire. One does not usually associate flowers with witchcraft, but for many centuries garlands were burned in bonfires on the eve of St John (June 23rd) with the object of banishing the evil sisterhood from the land. One of the last surviving customs of this type continues to be observed at this time of the year in the small village of St Cleer in Cornwall. A huge bonfire about thirty foot tall is set alight on a hilltop and while it burns herbs and flowers are cast into the flames in the presence of an audience drawn from every part of Cornwall, including a large number of holiday-makers. This ancient rite is calculated to keep witchcraft out of the village for a further year.

Midsummer Quit Rent. A quit rent consisting of a red rose is paid every Midsummer to the Lord Mayor of London by the Churchwarden of All Hallows. The flower rests on a cushion which is handed over with much ceremony at the Mansion House. The custom has been continuously carried out since the year 1346 when Sir Robert Knollys incurred a token fine for building an unauthorized footbridge in Seething Lane in the City of London. Payments of this character, which are valueless in terms of money, are also known as peppercorn rents, a peppercorn being an object of no worth.

In Cowper's *Table Talk* there is a poetic reference to this type of payment, which originated as a feudal due from a tenant to his lord:

> True, while they live, the courtly laureate pays
> His quit-rent ode, his peppercorn of praise.

Among what were once called Floral Services was the gift of a rose at Christmas and a snowball in summer to James V in return for certain lands granted by the monarch to the Haldane family of Scotland:

> Ye Haddens o' the Moor, ye pay nocht,
> But a harren tether of its socht,
> And a red rose at Yule, and a sno'b' at Lammas.

How this obligation was carried out remains one of the mysteries of folklore. A Yorkshire landowner, in emulation of the Scottish laird previously described, demanded from his tenant as rent a snowball in summer and a rose in winter. Until early in the present century a number of ancient tenures survived in Leicestershire under which land was held by presenting the owner with a peppercorn rent of a floral garland and three roses.

June 27: Royal Tour of London Gardens. About half a century ago it occurred to a number of dedicated flower lovers, including the late Lord Noel Buxton, that the window boxes of London, especially in the drearier areas, deserved special recognition and encouragement. To that end the London Gardeners' Society and its many affiliated bodies have held flower shows and competitions for an All London trophy every year. Queen Elizabeth the Queen Mother, who is notably a great flower lover and patron of the London Gardeners' Society, tours the small gardens of London each June, the climax of this activity being the All London Garden Championship which is held annually in the last week of July. Cups and similar awards are given as prizes for the most attractive window boxes on display in the City.

July 8th: Burry Man. Each July on the day prior to the opening of South Queensferry's Annual Fair, an extraordinary character known as the Burry Man appears in the streets of this Scottish town. Covered from head to foot in a close-fitting suit comprised of the burrs of the thistle and teasel, he is greeted everywhere with great affability by the residents who make him presents of money. There is an old superstition locally that a donation to the Burry Man brings good luck.

The Burry Man wears a floral head-dress which completely conceals his face and carries flower-decked staves. Who he is and what is the origin of this curious custom remains a mystery, but it is known that a Burry Man has walked the streets of South Queensferry every July for the past six hundred years.

July: Bawming the Thorn. Appleton in Cheshire holds a "Bawming (decorating) the Thorn" ritual early in July, when a ceremonial dance takes place around a hawthorn tree which is believed to have originated as a cutting from the Holy Thorn of Glastonbury. The local folk then parade through the town, after which the tree is garlanded by children with floral wreaths and spring flowers. The custom, which is very ancient, may represent the maypole dance in its old form as it was practised many centuries ago.

July: Rush-Bearing Ceremony. On the last Saturday in July, or alternatively the first in August, a rush-bearing procession takes place at Ambleside in Westmorland before large numbers of onlookers. In the past when the custom was more general, the ceremony took place on the day of the church's dedication, when reeds or rushes were carried into the building and spread on the floor to serve as a primitive carpet for the greater comfort of the worshippers.

> This day when forth by rustic music led
> The village children while the sky is red
> With evening lights advance in long array

Through the still churchyard each with garland gay
To the wide church door
Charged with the offerings their fathers bore
For decoration in the papal time.

This ritual also survives at Kendal in Westmorland, and there the children wear flowers in their hair. In the old days at Glossop, Derbyshire, the wakes cart loaded with rushes and decorated with flowers, passed along the street preceded by dancers and the local band. Rushes and flowers were then brought into the church and suspended in the chancel.

August: Minden Roses. During the Seven Years War a crushing defeat was inflicted on the French army in the Battle of Minden which was fought in Germany on August 1st, 1759, a year when the roses bloomed in profusion. The British forces marched into the guns of the enemy, snatching up rose blossoms and attaching these to their coats, hats and equipment as they did so. They then fired a volley which drove the French in confusion from the battlefield. On the anniversary of this famous battle the regiments which participated celebrate the occasion by wearing red and yellow roses in their caps. Their colours and drums are similarly decorated.

August: Eisteddfod Acorn Crown. The Royal National Eisteddfod which is held in the first week of August is a revival of an ancient national festival dating from as early as the sixth century. Eisteddfod means "the session of the Bards of the Isles of Britain", and is based on the Welsh "Eistedd" to sit. The revived musical festival is a bardic and poetic contest which is proclaimed annually by the Arch Druid who wears a copper breastplate and a coronet of oak leaves, the oak leaf being one of the emblems of Jupiter.

September: First Fruits of the Harvest. Each September the gathering of the "first fruits of the harvest" is commemorated at Richmond in a ceremony in which a sample of the season's crop plus a bottle of wine is presented to the Mayor of this Yorkshire town. The celebration of the first fruits was once an essential feature of the harvest season, but has been replaced by the religious-style harvest festival introduced by the Reverend Stephen Hawker in 1843, when he invited churchgoers at Morwenstowe in Cornwall to partake of "the bread of the new corn". Hawker was a famous character, if something of an eccentric. He is known to have dressed as a mermaid and serenaded his parishioners from an offshore rock.

September: Painswick Ceremony. On the Sunday closest to the Feast of the Nativity the parishioners of Painswick in Gloucestershire perambulate the boundaries of their church singing hymns and old-time songs. This ceremony is known as "clipping", which means embracing. Local children carrying garlands of flowers then dance round the churchyard. The origins of the clipping ceremony are unclear although it is possibly based on a rite inherited from Roman times.

September: St Giles' Fair. One of the most enjoyable floral displays in Britain accompanies the Barnstaple, Devon, St Giles' Fair held every September, which has been described as among the most colourful and interesting fairs in the West Country. The ceremonies include the garlanding of the Guildhall with brightly coloured ribbons and flowers.

October 21st: Trafalgar Day. Trafalgar Day commemorates the Battle of Trafalgar which saw both victory over the French and the death of Admiral Lord Nelson on that day in 1805. From October 21st 1895 onwards a wreath of bays has been placed annually on the plinth of the Nelson Column in London's Trafalgar Square, and at Portsmouth H.M.S. *Victory*, Nelson's flag ship, is similarly garlanded. Bay leaves were used in classical times as decorations for heroes and victors in battle. Nelson remains a living force in Britain's Navy where the phrase "Nelson is not dead" is still used.

October 31st: Hallowe'en. And now we have reached the twilight of the floral year, All Hallows' Eve or Hallowe'en, which occurs at the same time as Samhain, a forgotten festival which opened the Celtic year. Apart from the ceremonial bonfires which were lit at this time and which have over the centuries been deferred for a week to form part of the Guy Fawkes celebrations, there are a number of customs involving apples which take place at the Hallowe'en party. Apples are bobbed for in tubs or suspended from the ceiling by lengths of string. A girl who looks at her reflection in a mirror by candlelight at midnight, having an apple in her hand, may expect to see the image of her husband-to-be looking back at her from the glass. It is certain that these rituals are remnants of the celebrations associated with Pomona, the Roman Goddess of Fruit Trees who was one of the divinities of Autumn.

The Hallowe'en rites take various forms in the British Isles and elsewhere. At Hinton St George the children visit the houses demanding candles. These are then placed in lanterns made from mangolds and used to illuminate the procession which marches along the village street.

November 11th: Remembrance Sunday. Annually, on November 11th, huge crowds gather in Whitehall to see wreaths laid at the Cenotaph, the memorial to the dead of two World Wars. Following the sounding of the Last Post the Queen places her own wreath of Flanders poppies on the base of the memorial, and is followed by the high officers of State with their floral tributes. Flanders poppies are made by disabled ex-service men to commemorate those who died in Flanders, the scene of such dreadful carnage in World War I. The red poppy is a well-known emblem of sleep, and also the symbol of consolation.

December: The Christmas Feast. At the season of goodwill the birth of Jesus Christ is celebrated in a festival which was superimposed by the church upon an earlier feast held in honour of the sun. Now the evergreen is king, the holly, the ivy and the mistletoe holding pride of place within the home. The streets of towns and cities are likewise decorated to remind all that life lives on in nature even though the flowers might have vanished from the fields.

To appreciate the festival in all its floral glory a church should be visited during the twelve days of Christmas to see the decorations which are triumphs of artistry. It will be noted, however, that the mistletoe is not among them, for it was once an emblem of Druidism, the religion of the Celts.

At Christmas time many inns are decorated with garlands, a

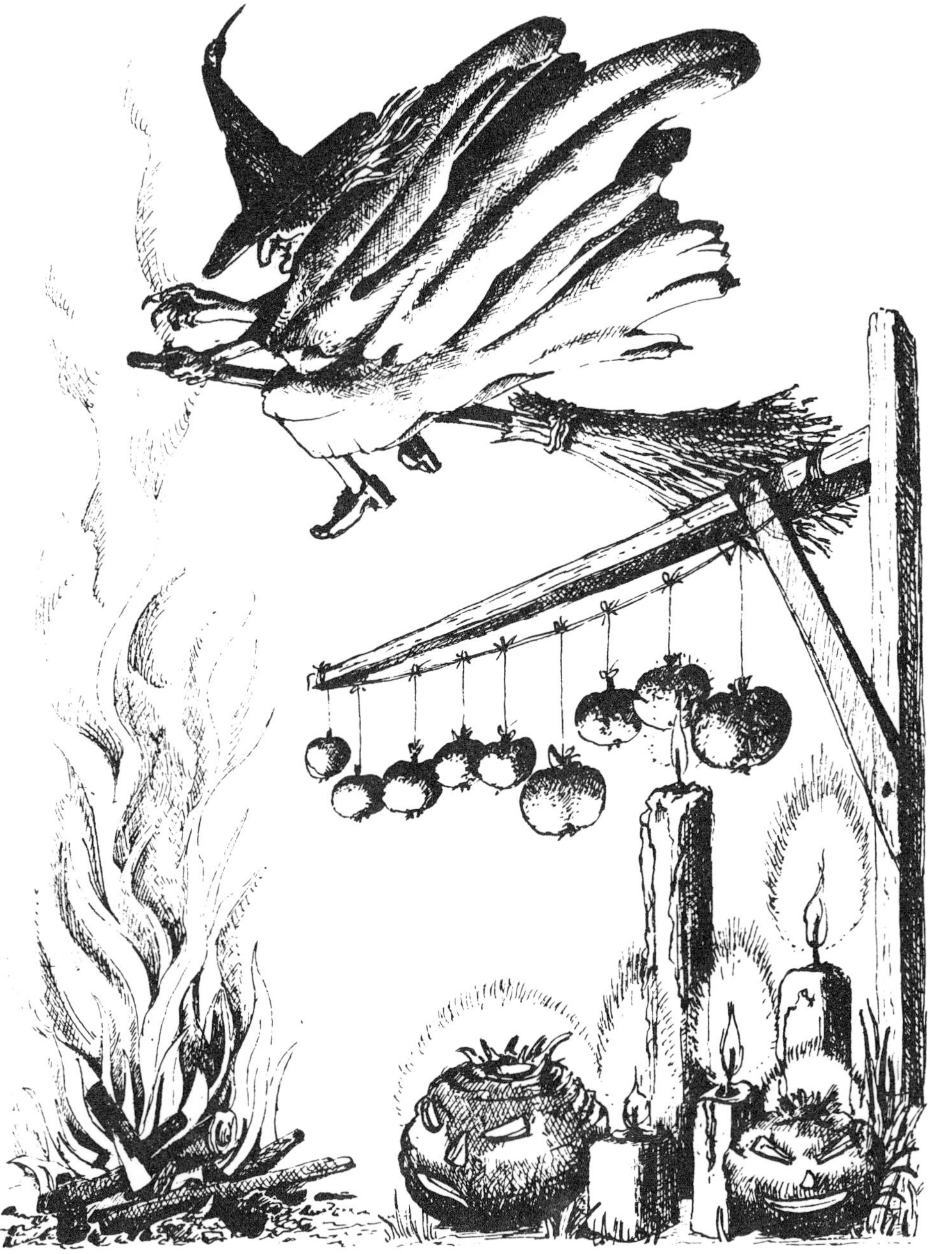

Flight of Fancy

custom which originated in the display of a bush outside a tavern to indicate that wine was sold within.

The highlight of the London Christmas season is the setting up of a giant Christmas tree in Trafalgar Square. The tree, an annual gift from Norway, is decked with lights that are ceremonially lit by the Mayor of Westminster as a symbol of goodwill to all nations and all creeds.

CHAPTER ELEVEN

Flowers in Poetry and Song: Fact and Fancy

For as long as poetry has existed, it has been influenced by nature. Every poet is a word colourist, and the countryside is his palette. What could be more emotionally stirring than this verse by M. R. Brown:

> 'Twas in a glorious eastern isle
> Where the acacias lightly move,
> Their snowy wreaths where sunbeams smile
> Brightly and scorchingly, like love,
> . . . where roses blossom through the year
> And palms their green plumed branches rear.

Flowers form a major element in the word-painter's imagery as in Richardson's:

> In every breathing bloom I find
> Some pleasing emblem of thy mind.
> The blushes of the op'ning rose
> Thy tender modesty disclose.

William Shakespeare drew constantly upon floral motifs for his poems and plays, especially in *The Winter's Tale* which was written at a time when the Bard occupied his spare hours in the cultivation of flowers at his Stratford home. In Shakespeare's day town and country were so closely interlinked that flowers, plants and trees provided a cultural setting for the great majority of English people.

Sir, the year growing ancient
Not yet on summer's death, nor on the birth
Of trembling winter, – the fairest flowers o' the season
Are our carnations, and streak'd gillyvors.

Then there is that favourite of all lovers of springtime, the daffodil:

When daffodils begin to peer, –
With hey! the doxy over the dale, –
Why, then comes in the sweet o' the year;

Shakespeare associates the marigold, under its old name Mary-bud, with the sunrise in these lines from *Cymbeline*:

Hark! hark! the lark at heaven's gate sings,
And Phoebus 'gins arise,
His steeds to water at those springs
On chalic'd flowers that lies;
And winking Mary-buds begin
To ope their golden eyes:

Shakespeare was a countryman at heart which is why we find so many references to wild flowers in his plays. In fact no true *Midsummer-Night's Dream* would be complete without such delightful lines as:

And in the woods where often you and I
Upon faint primrose beds were wont to lie.

The cowslip, an oft-mentioned Shakespearian flower, was a favourite with the Elizabethans. In *A Midsummer-Night's Dream* we learn of

The cowslips tall her pensioners be
In their gold coats spots you see.

possibly inspired by the handsome young attendants, known as the gentlemen pensioners, who accompanied Queen Elizabeth I and her court wherever she travelled.

And there is a poetic allusion to the dewdrop as a solidified pearl, which is one of the oldest superstitions we have inherited:

I must go seek some dew drops here
And hang a pearl in every cowslip's ear.

Like Shakespeare, Edmund Spenser was a word-colourist of great power who drew upon the imagery provided by flowers:

Seest how fresh my flowers been spread,
Dyed in lily white and crimson red
With leaves ingrained in rustic green,
Colours meet to cloathe a maiden queen.

Edmund Spenser also penned this allegory, drawn from the most sensitive of trees, the aspen, which according to Christian belief has trembled from shame ever since Judas hanged himself from one of its branches:

His hand did quake
And tremble like an aspen green,
And troubled blood through his pale face was seen
To come and go, with tydings from the heart.

Green, the emblem of Spring and verdure, seems to have fascinated the older generation of poets, for it was the symbol of abundance, of eternal life and fertility, and despite its unlucky aspect as the colour worn by the fairy folk it continues to be beloved by the poets. Ovid, the Roman poet, equated green with youth:

And as eternal youth is mine, thou also shalt
be always green and thy leaf know no decay.

However, green could have a sinister symbolism as the emblem of jealousy, hence these lines from Shakespeare's *Othello*:

O! beware, my lord, of jealousy;
It is the green-ey'd monster which doth mock
The meat it feeds on . . .

One of the most interesting poets of the floral world was the seventeenth-century French Jesuit René Rapin whose work had a profound influence upon that English "man of the trees", the diarist John Evelyn. Rapin, who seems to have concentrated upon the mystical aspect of plant and flower life and particularly the classical legends, described the metamorphosis of a maid into a violet in the following graceful lines:

Next from the Vi'let choice perfumes exhale
She now disguised in a blue dusty veil
Springs through the humble grass an humble flow'r,
Her stature little and her raiment poor.
If truth in ancient poems is conveyed
This modest flower was once a charming maid.
Her name Ianthus, of Diana's train.
The brightest nymph that ever graced a plain . . .

The pansy was another of the flowers which inspired Rapin. He described it as "the flower of Jove":

With all the beauties in the valleys bred
Spearmint that's born with myrtle crowns to wed
And Jove's own flower, in which three colours meet
To rival Violets, though without their sweet.

The ranunculus provided further inspiration for this remarkable priest whose affection for the flowers of garden and field seems to have possessed a decidedly pagan quality:

Ranunculus who with melodious strains
Once charmed the ravished nymph on Libyan plains,
Now boasts through verdant fields his rich attire
Whose love-sick look betrays a secret fire . . .

Another almost forgotten poet who once sang the praises of flowers was Erasmus Darwin, grandfather of Charles Darwin, the author of *The Origin of Species*. Erasmus, a radical free-thinker and fiery temperance advocate, possessed an eight-acre botanical garden which testified to the softer side of his nature. His curious *Loves of the Plants*, published in 1789 as part of his work *The Botanic Garden*, contains some interesting verse dedicated to the Barometz, a fern growing in Tartary which belongs to the genre of Fabulous Plants:

Cradled in snow and fanned by arctic air
Shines gentle Barometz, thy golden hair
Rooted in earth, each cloven hoof descends,
And round and round each flexile neck she bends . . .

Eccentricities aside, one finds pleasure in returning to poetry more appropriate to the flowery theme, in the gentler verse of

Shelley on the narcissus:

And Narcissi, the finest among them all
Who gaze upon their eyes in the stream's recess
Till they die of their own dear loveliness

an obvious allusion to the death from self-love of the youth Narcissus in the classical legend.

Sir Walter Scott paid tribute to the violet with his poem of that name:

The violet in her greenwood bower,
Where birchen boughs with hazels mingle,
May boast itself the fairest flower
In glen, or copse, or forest dingle.

Wordsworth says of the daisy: "we meet thee like a pleasant thought" and Montgomery reminds us that:

There is a flower, a little flower,
With silver crest and golden eye
That welcomes every changing hour
And weathers every sky.

Charlotte Smith, the nineteenth-century novelist who enjoyed a considerable reputation in her day appears to have been fascinated by the concept of flowers as time-keepers, hence her poem "Floras Horologe", inspired by the discovery of the great Linneaus that flowers opened and closed their petals at fixed times.

In every copse and sheltered dell
Unveiled to the observant eye
Are faithful monitors who tell
How pass the hours and seasons by.
The green robed children of the spring
Will mark the periods as they pass,
Mingle with leaves time's feathered wing
And bind with flowers his silent grass.

She concludes:

Thus in each flower and simple bell
That in our path betrodden lie
Are sweet remembrancers which tell
How fast the winged moments fly.

The violet in her green-
wood bower,

Where birchen boughs with
hazels mingle,

May boast itself the fairest
flower

In glen, or copse, or forest
dingle.

Sir Walter Scott

Both Tennyson in "The Princess" and Tom Moore in "Paradise and The Peri" pay tribute to the water lily, the first with:

> Now folds the lily all her sweetness up
> And slips into the bosom of the lake.
> So fold thyself, my dearest, thou and slip
> Into my bosom and be lost in me.

Tom Moore saw the flowers as:

> Those virgin lilies all the night
> Bathing their beauties in the lake
> That they may rise more fresh and bright
> When their beloved sun's awake.

In philosophical mood the poet Robert Burns compared the frailty of the poppy to the transient happiness of life:

> Pleasures are like poppies spread,
> You seize the flower the bloom is shed.

Poetic moralizing came readily to the tongue and pen of the sentimental flower lovers of that older generation, hence its predominance in epigram and homily. Lucy Larcomb on the golden rod:

> Because its sun-shaped blossoms show
> How souls receive the light of God
> And unto earth give back that glow,
> I thank Him for the golden rod.

Roses are invariably entangled with thorns in epigrams and proverbs: "Every rose has its thorn"; "Without thorns no roses"; "He who would gather roses must not fear thorns". A modern Greek proverb reminds us "From the thorn springs the rose and from the rose the thorn".

Gardens stimulated a great deal of poetry, perhaps because they provided an oasis which could be completely insulated from the real world outside. William Cowper even fell in love with his greenhouse and sealed the compact with these lines:

> Who loves a garden, loves a greenhouse too.
> Unconscious of a less propitious clime
> There blooms exotic beauty warm and snug
> While the winds whistle and the snows descend.

Tom Hood in his "Plea of the Midsummer Fairies" describes a garden as

> . . . a shady and sequestered scene
> Like those famed gardens of Boccaccio
> Planted with his own laurels evergreen
> And roses that for endless summers blow;

Now for a few proverbs relating to gardens in general: "The garden is a lovely thing, God wot" from Thomas Edward the Manx poet, and the famous lines of the poetess Dorothy Frances Gurney:

> The kiss of the sun for pardon,
> The song of the birds for mirth.
> One is nearer God's heart in a garden
> Than anywhere else on earth.

Perhaps most interesting of all is the Hebrew saying: "What flowers are to gardens, spices to food, gems to a garment, and stars to heavens; such are proverbs interwoven in speech."

There is a catalogue of undesirable qualities taken from the proverbial lore of Spain. Nothing is apparently so demoralizing as "A garden without water, a house without a roof, a wife without love and a careless husband."

An entire branch of the art of poetry consists of rhymes recited by children in the course of playground games. The poems are extremely interesting in their own right and even more so when one considers that they have descended to the younger generation from adults over the centuries. One is a Cheshire quatrain dedicated to the ribwort plantain the flowers of which are black:

> Chimney sweeper all in black
> Go to the brook and wash your back.
> Wash it clean or wash it none,
> Chimney sweeper have you done?

Again the well-known nursery rhyme:

> Mary, Mary, quite contrary,
> How does your garden grow?
> With cockle shells and silver bells,
> And pretty maids all in a row.

This is almost certainly a reference to the garden variety of the *Saxifraga granulata* which has the folk name Pretty Maids. This flower, which is now confined to rural areas, once flourished in London's Gray's Inn.

In the game called Three Flowers children chanted:

My mistress sent me unto thine
With three young flowers both fair and fine.
The Pink, the Rose and the Gillyflower.
And as they here do stand whilk will you sink,
Whilk will you swim
And whilk bring home to land.

A seasonal rhyme recited by children which makes reference to the daffodil is mentioned by Iona and Peter Opie in their work *The Lore and Language of Schoolchildren*:

Daffodils yellow
Daffodils gay
To put upon the table
On Easter Day.

Then again there is a May Day song belonging to the "children's calendar" of events:

Buttercups and daisies.
Oh what pretty flowers,
Coming in the springtime
To tell of sunny hours.

In the children's lore of Cambridgeshire occurs a curious litany relating to divination using the clover:

A clover of two
A clover of two
The first boy or girl you meet
In field street or lane
You'll have one of his or her name.

Flowers provided one of the most popular themes in folk song, the following being constantly mentioned in the old ballads: the primrose, gillyflower, cowslip, marigold, violet, sweet-william, daisy and broom.

Flowers are frequently used to paint sombre epitaphs, remin-

Awakening Spring

ders of love which although dead remains undying. That epic folk poem "The Unquiet Grave" tells of the dead man who speaks to his still living sweetheart from the realms of death:

O don't you remember the garden grove
Where we used to walk?
Pluck the finest flower of them all
'T will wither to a stalk.

The flower motif also occurs in a description of that Other World beyond death, as in Retson's "Dead Man's Song":

The fields about the city fair
Were all with roses set.
Gillyflowers, and carnations fair
Which canker could not fret.

And there is the echo of an ancient mystical kinship between human beings and the plant world in the folk song "Fair Margaret and Sweet William":

And out from her mouth there sprung a rose
And out of his a briar.

Flowers, plants and trees have played such an immense part in human affairs covering the entire range of emotions from hope and love to mourning and death that it would be surprising if they had not become a major source of metaphor. For example, the word "flower" has been frequently used to describe cities and states. The ancient Middle Kingdom of China was known as The Flowery Kingdom, and Springfield, Illinois, in the United States, was called the Flower City because of the remarkable floral beauty of its suburbs, while Aranjes in Spain is known as the Metropolis of Flora.

And when it comes to great men, we have King Arthur, the sixth-century British chieftain renowned as the Flower of Kings; the warrior king of Liddesdale, Sir William Douglas, known as the Flower of Chivalry; and Geoffrey Chaucer, the Flower of the Poets. The island of Zante was the Flower of the Levant, an allusion to its remarkable natural beauty, and flowery phrases are called Flowers of Speech.

The employment of flowers to illustrate some attribute of the personality is a common practice, hence shrinking violet or wallflower for the timorous or retiring type. In some cases a particular flower has become the emblem of a great personage as, for example, the Emperor Napoleon Bonaparte who was known euphemistically as Corporal Violet, due to the fact that this happened to be his favourite flower. When he left France for exile in Elba the "Little Corporal" whispered to his followers that they could expect his return when the violets bloomed. During his absence, when his supporters were forced to operate in secret, they identified one another by the violets they wore as badges. True to his promise Napoleon arrived in Paris at the very time when there was an incredibly beautiful display of violets in the Tuileries. Later when he returned to exile, this time permanently, the restored Bourbon monarchy condemned as treasonable any attempt to display the violet in public or even to incorporate the flowers in a bouquet.

With the return to power of the Bonapartist dynasty the violet was once again in fashion, and as Napoleon the Little led his bride Eugénie to the altar she was offered a cluster of violets by a market woman from the street.

The forget-me-not, like the roses of the great English Civil War, has secured a niche in history. When Henry of Lancaster was in exile his followers wore the forget-me-not as an emblem of loyalty, and during the reign of Edward IV the flower was displayed in enamel on the knight's collar of gold.

There is a little known tradition associated with that fascinating blossom the snowdrop, or February Fair Maid as it is sometimes called. During the Crimean War the allied soldiers encamped before Sebastopol suffered terribly from an extremely cruel winter even for Russia. Eagerly they looked for some sign of returning spring, and then on a day in icy February one of them discovered three white blossoms – the first snowdrops of the year. He and his comrades stood reverently before the flowers with uncovered heads. On returning home at the end of the war they brought with them the bulbs of the Crimean snowdrop which as a result became established in Britain.

The powerful influence of military discipline is emphasized by a curious tradition which survived until comparatively recent times in Russia. In the eighteenth century the Empress Catherine ordered a soldier to stand guard over a rose bush in the gardens of Tsar-skoe selo near St Petersburg. The custom was maintained until well into the present century, although no flowers remained there to guard.

Modern readers may be surprised to discover that the poppy, in this case the opium poppy, was the cause of a war between Great Britain and the Chinese in the nineteenth century. An attempt to force the Chinese population to purchase supplies of Indian opium led to a conflict which lasted from 1839 until 1842, and as a direct consequence of this shameful affair the secret empire of the Chinese was opened up to the West for the first time in history.

The oldest national flower on record is the Scottish thistle, the tradition having originated, it is believed, as the outcome of a battle with the Danes. The latter, hoping to take the Scots unawares, had crept stealthily towards the Scottish camp, and might have succeeded had not one man trod on a thistle with his bare foot. He gave a loud cry of pain which awakened the slumbering Scots who succeeded in driving the attackers out of their country with great carnage. In another account of the adoption of the thistle by the Scots, we are told that it was decided in the middle of the fifteenth century to substitute the thistle for the figure of St Andrew on the national banner, its symbolic meaning being "nobody provokes me with impunity". The Most Ancient Order of the Thistle was founded by James V of Scotland. The thistle is by no means a popular plant. Its first mention in literature was in the Bible where it formed part of the primal curse upon mankind.

The people of the United States are extremely fond of flower emblems; it was in fact California which first adopted a flower as its symbol, in this case the golden poppy which grows wild throughout the state.

This interest in flowers seems to have overcome Puritan prejudice in New England where the children were forbidden to play with their toys on the Sabbath. The little ones adroitly solved the problem by making small "Sunday dolls" with red petticoats made of poppies they gathered in the meadows.

Prejudice can take strange forms. The ancient Greeks believed that no virtuous woman would ever appear in public wearing a dress with a floral motif, this being the familiar badge of the harlot. The Laws of the Athenian statesman Solon enforced this rule. To quote Clemens the Alexandrian:

As fugitive slaves are known by their stigmata
So flowered garments indicate one of the demi-monde.

So much has been written concerning the rose that it is sometimes difficult to discover any out-of-the-way aspect to bring before the reader, but it may be of interest to learn that well over a century ago there was formed in Paris a group of literary men who called themselves "The Society of The Rose". To qualify for membership it was necessary to have written a song about roses which found favour with the other members. The meeting-place of The Society of the Rose was known appropriately as "The Thicket of Roses". And another curious fact from history: the Roman historian Pliny held the view that England derived the name Albion not so much from the whiteness of its chalk cliffs, but from the masses of white roses which grew upon them. The Romans associated the name Albion with the Latin *albul* (white).

As a token of respect for the great Conservative prime minister Benjamin Disraeli, Lord Beaconsfield, members of his party wear a primrose on the anniversary of his death under the impression that this was his favourite flower. Disraeli's pet flower was in fact the dahlia. The error arose because Queen Victoria sent primroses to lay on "Dizzy's" grave accompanied by a card bearing the words "His favourite flower". Her Majesty was, however, making a sentimental gift on behalf of her late husband, the Prince Consort, who adored primroses.

CHAPTER TWELVE

What's In A Name?

Any man who walketh the mead
In bud, or blade or bloom may find
A meaning suited to his mind.

Tennyson

Our plant names have a curious history for they were frequently derived from the languages of peoples from far off lands, including the Latins and Greeks, the Celts, the Anglo-Saxons and the Norse. Many such names originated in the Middle East, particularly in Arabia and Persia.

Wherever the overseas raider or colonist settled in these isles we discover plant names of Scandinavian or Germanic origin. Swedish and Danish names are extremely common in the north of England. The manner by which plants and flowers both domestic and wild obtained their names also provides – dare we use the term – a potted history of the evolution of ideas about nature over the centuries, and also illustrates the whimsicality of our ancestors from whom the stories have descended.

A number of quite different factors may have determined the choice of a particular name. For example it could be based upon a fancied resemblance to some other object, as we have seen in the case of the dandelion.

Because the word rue means "repentance", this flower (*Ruta graveolens*) became known as the Herb of Grace – repentance being necessary to obtain the grace of God. It is referred to in

Hamlet as "Herb o' Grace o' Sundays". Rue was employed in exorcisms during the Middle Ages – priests sprinkling holy water upon the possessed with a bunch of rue. And as the January 18th birthday flower the plant symbolizes "grace, mercy, pity, purification and bitterness".

The word "hybrid", which we use in connection with flowers, is borrowed from the Latin *hybrida,* used to describe the offspring of a domestic cow and a wild boar, a species which in ancient times roamed throughout Europe. There is also an animal association with the word "branch", which has its origins in *branca* meaning paw. "Twig" is based on the root *twi,* meaning a forked shape.

Taking a number of flower names alphabetically we discover some extremely interesting examples of the process of name formation.

Acanthus, the leaves of which have a spiny pattern, comes from the Greek *akathenta* meaning thorn.

Anemone is derived from *anemos,* the Greek word for wind.

Aster, with its fancied resemblance to a star, is from the Latin *aster* for star.

Camellia is from Kamel, the priest of that name who introduced this plant into Europe from the East in the seventeenth century.

Canterbury bells have a direct allusion to the pre-Reformation pilgrimage to Canterbury and the harness bells which jingled merrily from the pilgrims' horses as they passed along the Pilgrim's Way.

Clematis originated with the Greek word *klematis,* from *klema* or vine branch, which seems obvious when we consider that the clematis is a plant which entwines itself along a convenient wall.

Unhappy memories of childhood mishaps are revived from the study of the name of the *Cowslip,* for it is based on *Cu* for cow and *Slyppe* or slime, a reminder that cows usually leave their signatures where the cowslips grow.

Crocus means yellow; in fact to be strictly correct the name should be restricted to a flower with a saffron hue.

Daisy comes from the old English word 'Day's Eye' which was inspired by the sunlike centre of this ever welcome spring flower.

Gentian, which grows in mountainous areas (the Swiss Alps and the American Rockies), is based on Gentius, an ancient king of Illyria on the Adriatic coast, who was defeated by the Romans.

Gladiolus. The name of this plant is a reminder of the gladiatorial combats fought in the arenas of ancient Rome. The spikes of the flowers bore fancied resemblance to the gladus, which was the name of the sword carried by the combatants.

Jonquil or Little Rush. The pronunciation of the name has changed in recent times; in the past it was called Junkwill. However, with poetic licence Wordsworth decided to improve it, hence its present name of Jonquil.

Larkspur is so called due to an imagined resemblance between its spur-shaped flowers and the hind claw of a lark.

Lilac means blue. Originally the Persians called it Nilack, the Arabs Laylak and last of all came the Spanish who called it Lilac.

Lobelia is from Mathias de Lobel, a Flemish botanist, and *Magnolia* from Pierre Magnol, another botanist.

Nasturtium has a pungent perfume, hence the name which is based on the Latin *nasus* (nose) and *torqueo* (twist); a nose-twisting plant with a tongue-twisting name.

Orchid comes from *orchis* the Greek word for testicle which its roots are supposed to resemble. The Romans used the orchid as the base of an aphrodisiac to which were added such horrors as spiders, crickets and blister beetles to increase the power.

Pansy means "thoughtful", the name having originated from *pensée*, the French word for thoughtfulness.

There is a strong religious symbolism in the *passion flower*, which represents the instruments of the Passion of our Lord Jesus Christ.

Petunia is a flower name which came into vogue with the discovery of the tobacco plant in the New World. Because of the resemblance between its violet and white flowers with those of the tobacco plant *Petun*, this name was chosen.

Poinsett was the name of a diplomat in South Carolina who, while acting as special minister to Mexico in the nineteenth century, discovered the large flaming flowers which were given the name *Poinsettia*.

Syringa has musical connotations for the word means "reed". It was chosen because its stems were used for the reed "Pan pipes" of the ancient musicians.

Salad Days

Thyme is from *thymos* and is connected with *thyos*, the Greek word for incense.

Tulip comes from the word turban, the flowers being somewhat similar in appearance to the Turkish headgear. *Tulbend* is the Turkish for turban.

Verbena in Roman times meant "sacred bough". These boughs were borne by Roman heralds when they were charged with delivering a declaration of war or a demand for some other form of satisfaction.

The *Wistaria* is named after Caspar Wistar, a "professor of anatomy, midwifery and surgery" in Pennsylvania in the early years of the nineteenth century.

Zinnia is from J. C. Zinn, an eighteenth-century botanist.

It is when we turn to the wild flowers, the blossoms of field and hedgerow that delight young children and all who enjoy country life, that we discover how really interesting the names of flowers can be. While many flowers relate to ancient gods and that magical world of elves, fairies and witches, a number possess other meanings which readers may find intriguing.

The coltsfoot has leaves which suggest the hooves of a colt. It is also called calve's foot, ass's foot, colt herb and sow's foot. Sometimes country folk burn the stems and inhale the smoke to cure a cough for which reason it is also known as cough wort.

Among the curious country names given to the anemone, or windflower, we find bread and cheese and cider, chimney smock, moon flower, smell foxes and smell smock.

The five-petalled dog violet is one of the most welcome plants of early spring. The word "dog" was usually employed by our ancestors to designate some object or plant of an inferior character; in this case it was the sweet violet.

Another spring flower, the primrose, is not a rose, its name being a corruption of the French word *promerole*. However, the children of Caithness call it the buckle-faalie; those of Devon the butter rose, while in the Shetlands it is known as the May pink. In Yorkshire it is called simmerin from the Norwegian *kusymre* or cow anemone.

Now let us consider a number of whimsical flower names which provide an intriguing vista into the thought process of flower lovers in the past.

Alleluiah is the wood-sorrel and means "praise the Lord". It is so called because it was supposed to have been in flower at the time of the Resurrection of Jesus Christ.

Baa lambs are not as one would suppose sheep, but little white clovers, doubtless so named because of their fluffy appearance.

Bad man's oatmeal is shepherd's purse, a plant most unpopular among farmers because it takes much-needed sustenance from the soil.

Beggar's blanket, sometimes called Adam's blanket, is the folk name of the great mullein which has soft leaves. It is also called bunny's ears and fluff weed.

Billy buttons is the popular name for the marsh marigold because of its similarity to a button. Blindy buffs are far from funny, however, for these are the scarlet poppies which tradition asserts send you blind if you hold them too close to the eyes. Equally erroneous is the old belief that if the poppy is held to the ear it brings on an attack of ear-ache.

Bobby hood is one of the names of the red campion; it has five red petals which at first sight look like ten since each is almost cut in two. It is also called poor Robin, cock Robin and Robin Hood. The name is derived from Robin Goodfellow, one of the fairy folk we find in William Shakespeare.

The Scots and those living in northern England often call ladies smock bog spinks; and their children know them as lamb's lakins which means lamb's playthings. Ladies smock, however, is better known as bird's eye since the flower is decorated with a very small eye.

Bullock's eyes is a country name for the house leek which, come to think of it, does sometimes have the appearance of a staring eye. It is also called Jupiter's eye and Jupiter's beard because the bristly edges of the leaves resemble a bearded human chin. Scots folk often call this plant the hockery topner, the meaning of which is lost in the Celtic twilight.

The ribwort plantain is so called because the veins on its leaves are marked like ribs; it is also known as dog's rib.

The wild pansy or heart's-ease has a number of saucy folk names including cuddle-me-to-you, tittle-my-fancy and kiss-me-at-the-garden-gate. The romantic allusions could have arisen because the flower is said to have been pierced by Cupid's arrow in the days of old.

Now let us look at a number of flowers, weeds and plants

which are associated in one way or another with animals, birds and insects, etc.

There are cat's claws, cat's eyes, cat's faces, cat's milk and a cat's foot. There are dog's ears, dog's mouth, dog fingers, dog's ribs and dog's toes and the dog stinker, not to forget the dog-violet already mentioned.

Mice are represented in the mouse-ear, and mouse-tail; and rabbits by rabbit flower, rabbits, rabbit's chops, and rabbit's meat; while hares occur in the form of harebell, hare's beard, hare's eye and hare's meat.

For horse lovers there is the horse daisy, horse gold, horse-gowan, horse hoof, horse knobs and horse pennies. The prefix "horse", like that of "dog", indicates that it is of lowly status.

We have already mentioned the cowslip, but there are also cows and calves, cow-parsnip, cow's mouth, cow's eyes, cow's lick and cow slap.

Pigs are not forgotten in this catalogue of floral animality, for we have pig nots, pig's bubbles, pig's cole, pig's ears, pig's eye, pig's foot, pig's parsnip and pigweed, sow foot, sow-thistle and sow tits.

Now we turn to the kingdom of the birds which seems to have established diplomatic relations with the realm of flowers long ago if some of the names have any real significance.

Ornithologists who keep their eyes to the ground will discover such unsuspected species as bird's-eye, bird's-foot, bird's-tongue, cock flowers, cocks, cocks and hens, cockscombs, cocksfoot, cock's-head and cranesbill, crow's-foot, crow's-claws, and crow's-toes, not to forget cuckoo meat, cuckoo-pint, and such delights as cuckoo's bread and cuckoo's bread and cheese; to complete the picture there are to be found cuckoo's shoes and stockings.

Poultry farmers will no doubt be familiar with fighting cocks and the gandi gosling, also the goosebill, goose-grass, goose tongue, goosie-gander, gosling-grass, hen and chickens and hen-bane; Jenny Wren, nightingales, old owl, poor Robin, red Robin, Robin in the hedge, Robin run round the hedge and Robin red-breast's cushions should also be added to the list.

One could continue almost indefinitely on the theme of unusual flower names which had been inspired in the first place by an imagined resemblance to forms of life belonging to the animal kingdom.

Our reptiles and amphibia are also represented in toadflax, viper's bugloss and adder's flower. And insects with earwig, nit clickers, lousewort, butterfly bush and the bee flower.

Turning to flowers where the names relate to human beings we find many curious examples: bad man's posies, butcher boys, ladies' cushions, ladies' hatpins, ladies' thimbles, mother-breaks-her-heart, old man's beard, old man's woozard, old wives' tongues, king's nobs, Queen Mary's thistles, Prince's feathers, ragged Jack, shaggy Jack, tickling Tommies, white man's foot, wild williams and widow's wail.

Then, to clothe the people, there are flowers with such names as sun bonnets, shoes and stockings, princess robe, ragged shirt, old man's nightshirts, old woman's bonnet, gipsy's hats, gipsy's umbrella, granny's nightcap, devil's nightcap, devil garters and blue buttons.

We conclude with some very odd names indeed before returning to the more serious aspects of the folklore of flowers: arse-mart, Betty-go-to-bed-at-noon, love-in-a-tangle, fat bellies, naked Nanny and naughty man's plaything.

Although our treatment of the flower names of British folklore has been light-hearted, it should not be thought that the names borne by the flowers, trees and shrubs of the countryside are unimportant. In fact they embody ideas and beliefs which indicate clearly that in the pre-scientific era a rough and ready system of classification existed which rendered the recognition of plants relatively easy.

A whole world of old-time attitudes is reflected in the terms used to describe plants and flowers. They have been named after their discoverers, after the fairy folk, and after saints and sinners. As Thistleton-Dyer says in his book on the folklore of plants: "Could we penetrate to the original suggestive idea that called forth the name it would bring valuable information about the first openings of the human mind towards nature, and the mere dream of such a discovery invests with a strange charm, the words, that could tell, if we could understand so much of the forgotten infancy of the human race."

CHAPTER THIRTEEN

Earth and Stones

There have always been people to whom the word "soil" possesses a magical quality. This love for the soil is expressed in a number of well-known sayings like "blood and soil". We describe a person who is engaged in agriculture as a son of the soil. Earth, too, has a connotative ring. "The earth is the Lord's and the fulness thereof . . ." (Corinthians) is a reminder that the process of planting, growing and harvesting is an aspect of spiritual life. Earth was the great mother whom our ancestors worshipped in days gone by. In mythology the earth goddess was the wife of the sky god, and in Christian metaphor the union of Christ with his bride the Church represents the marriage of the earth with heaven. For earth is the great nourisher, the container of life and wealth, as it is the clay or dust to which all must return when life ends.

The joy of delving into the earth, planting and sowing with the hope of ultimately reaping is built into the nature of mankind. Those who own a garden are often aware of a serenity that is difficult to describe; a happiness that makes amends for the trials and tensions of the working day. Many whose lives are fraught with emotional stress, which in some circumstances could lead to a nervous breakdown, confess that gardening relieves the mind from the bonds which so often reduce life to a drudgery.

Digging can be one of the pleasures of life for many; indeed, turning over the earth is a creative act. There is an anonymous inscription in Melrose Abbey which reads:

Garden Guardian

The earth goes on the earth glittering in gold.
The earth goes to the earth sooner than it would.
The earth builds on the earth castles and towers
The earth says to the earth all this is ours.

Our ancestors believed in the Four Elements, the division of all creation into four primary groups: air, fire, water and earth.

The magic of the earth gave rise to a large number of mystical ideas which have survived, almost unrecognized as superstitions. In some parts of the world a belief in the supernatural powers inherent in the soil survives even today. In Dahomey, Africa, the farmers marked the earth with magical symbols to ensure a successful harvest. Our Scandinavian ancestors laid their newborn babies on the earth so that its energies could pass into their bodies. There is also a superstition which says that if a dying person is placed gently on the earth he will breathe his last within moments and be speedily freed from the agonies of death.

Turning to barbaric beliefs now happily rare, human sacrifices were once carried out by savages, (including our own ancestors) to propitiate the earth spirits, the blood being allowed to run freely into the ground. As recently as 1945 a man was discovered mysteriously murdered in a field in Warwickshire the victim of this type of ritual.

As one might expect, some of these old ideas continue to survive in the form of old wives' tales which are often the debased remnants of the ancient cult of earth worship.

Many country folk regard Mother Earth as a healer, and to cure a whitlow thrust the affected finger into the ground. A Leicestershire cure for rheumatism was to be buried naked in the garden for two hours at a time. Plasters of mud taken from marshy ground were believed to heal skin blemishes, and in the Shetlands a stitch could be cured by applying a plaster of churchyard earth to the spot. In Northumberland ringworm was remedied by rubbing the skin with garden mould and muttering a magical charm.

Barren soil is regarded by some people as evidence of a curse laid upon a particular plot of land by an evilly disposed witch. According to a similar tradition nothing grows upon the grave of a person who has been executed for a crime of which he or she is innocent.

In the Scillies the temporary grave of Sir Cloudesley Shovel, the admiral who wantonly exposed his ship and crew to danger and death, remains barren, it is said, as the direct result of the curse he laid upon himself by the unjust execution of a seaman.

There are other examples of the earth's barrenness arising as the result of the wicked behaviour of man. After the great battle at Ashingdon in Essex between Canute the Dane and Edmund Ironside the Saxon in A.D. 1016 no grass ever grew, it was said, upon a site so saturated with human blood.

Our ancestors regarded the earth as a kind of womb, and ploughing and sowing as a form of impregnation. These magical ideas continued to influence writers and artists right up to modern times. In the seventeenth century Francis Bacon maintained that in springtime, before the earth had expended its supernatural energies in the production of vegetables, it exhaled an odour which was both refreshing to the spirit and invigorating to the body. He added in all seriousness "ladies would do themselves much good by weeding".

A number of strange superstitions regarding grass circulated among rural cultivators in days gone by. A turf wrapped in a sheet of newspaper and laid on the breast of a corpse would protect the body from being whisked away by devils. In Gloucestershire a turf worn inside the hat counteracted a witch's spell, and in Cornwall country folk cured their warts by lying full length on the turf and crying out "Wart, wart, fly away".

Few gardeners are likely to become dedicated stone worshippers, but they could be interested in some of the curious beliefs inspired by pebbles in the past. There was once a strongly entrenched superstition that the pebbles which littered the fields and gardens actually grew there, this being the only logical explanation for their presence. It seemed self-evident at the time that the land had produced its own stones. Some held the view that the pebbles were the offspring of a "Mother Stone" or "Breeding Stone", being the seeds of the conglomerates which are often found in the countryside. At Blaxhall in Suffolk there is an immense boulder which local people insist was originally the size of a small loaf of bread. Visitors continue to travel great distances to see this phenomenon.

Yet another eccentric explanation given for the unceasing supply of pebbles which litter the vegetable and flower patch was that they had been dropped from the skies by the angels. One man, known to the author, made an immense collection of such stones which he considered far too sacred to be thrown away. Incidentally, if you discover a holed flint it should be treasured as it keeps off bad luck.

Eccentric theories and eccentrics are inseparable from land cultivation. How many sober citizens in the past have abandoned the comforts of domestic life for the rigours of a hermitage or commune in order to scratch a bare pittance from the soil? And old beliefs about plant life are revived with every generation. Man frequently turns to the romantic past when plants, like animals and human beings, were supposed to feel pleasure and suffer pain.

Many years ago the famous Indian scientist Sir Jagadis C. Bose carried out a number of experiments with plants which established to his own satisfaction that these respond to shock by registering a spasm. Bose became convinced that all living creatures, whether of the animal or vegetable kingdom, were united by a common bond of sympathy. He wrote: "Do not these records tell us of some property of matter common and persistent? That there is no break, but a uniform and continuous march of law.'

More recently, experimenters have claimed that flowers emit a "cry" when they need water; sounds that can be picked up by electrodes attached to the leaves. This takes us back to the earliest of the world's religious ideas when so-called primitive man believed that each plant, tree and flower possessed an indwelling spirit, which some might call the soul and others the mind.

CHAPTER FOURTEEN

The Flowering Year

Most of us are acquainted with the belief that it is dangerous to the sleeper's health to leave flowers in a bedroom at night. This fear, which is also shared by hospital nurses, is based on the curious doctrine that the scent exhaled by flowers after dark can be lethal for anyone whose vitality happens to be at a low ebb. The idea is, in fact, very old indeed and had its origins in the belief that evil spirits, or even the souls of the dead, lurked among the petals, from which they emerged under cover of darkness to attack the sleeper.

This ancient fear gave rise to serious concern in the not so distant past. Until well into the nineteenth century there was a prejudice among Londoners against flowers in places of entertainment, but rehabilitation was on its way as we read in a Victorian periodical: "Flowering flowers and shrubs are becoming more fashionable in our London ballrooms. No dread of noxious exhalations deters mamas from decorating their halls and staircases with flowers of every hue and fragrance, nor their daughters from braving the headaches and pale cheeks which are said to arise from such innocent and beautiful causes." The writer observed that flowers, exposed to overmuch human companionship, were liable to suffer abominably. "We remember seeing in the garden of a nurseryman at Brompton at the close of the London season, a squadron of plants in pots, withered and drooping and in some cases dead. We enquired of the gardener the cause of this floral decay. 'Why, Sir,' said the man, 'these plants have been out to so many parties during the season, that the heated rooms have almost killed them.'"

When we consider the immense importance of flowers in nature's scheme of things and further still the unending benefit they confer upon mankind, we begin to recognize the immense debt we owe to the silent jewels of the floral world.

Remembering also that plants supplied our first medicines, the very least the flower lover can do is to attend to the health of his flowers growing in his home and garden. The poet Robert Bridges may have said:

> I have loved flowers that fade
> Within whose magic tents
> Rich hues have marriage made
> With sweet unmemoried scents . . .

but we prefer to defer the fading process as long as possible once the blooms have been gathered, cut off in the prime of life, so to speak, and placed in a vase to beautify the room.

The art of flower preservation is quite as important as that of automobile maintenance, but arouses far less interest. To revive tulips and roses a piece of cotton (of the same colour as the flowers) should be gently tied around the petals, to give support and hold them together. They should be allowed to remain thus for several hours. In the case of delphiniums and larkspurs the best treatment is to add a little sugar to the water.

Chrysanthemums will often acquire a longer lease of life if about half an inch is cut from the stems. It is also advisable to plunge the freshly-cut stalks first into very hot water and then into cold. This hot and cold treatment proves an amazing stimulant for tired plants. Castor oil comes to the aid of ferns when they are a little off colour. A few drops must be added to the water and they should be left to soak overnight.

Even the best maintained flowers are doomed ultimately to pass away, but we can always resort to the botanical equivalent of embalmment to defer their entombment. Roses, marigolds and carnations preserve well. The Elizabethans became particularly skilled in the preservation of these flowers. Today the system they used in the sixteenth century is known to many flower lovers. Place the flowers in a cardboard box lined with sand and leave it in a hot airing cupboard until completely dry. Many other flowers seem to respond favourably to the same treatment.

Those planning to wax flowers should always use blossoms in mint condition. The leaves must be trimmed from the stem and to this is attached a small looped wire with which they can be suspended for twenty-five minutes or so in a temperature of 65°. This normally evaporates any remaining moisture. The blooms are then completely immersed in a wax which has been liquefied in a saucepan. The flowers are suspended once again by a fine wire and kept in a cool cupboard until the wax has set.

Flowers can also be employed for infusions (seeping or soaking them in liquid to extract their essences). In the case of hollyhocks, first remove the blossoms, dry them thoroughly in a shady place (never in sunshine) and keep them in a paper bag. For roses, the petals have to be removed and spread upon a table in the shade. Those intending to prepare infusions from marshmallows should pick the flowers before sunrise.

It is not generally realized that daffodils can be dangerous to the skin, causing eruptions and sometimes an unpleasant rash on the skin if they are handled too much.

The following flowers are dangerous if placed in the mouth, therefore children should be duly warned against them: aconites, anemones, laburnum and tulips.

We have seen how flowers were used sentimentally as love tokens, and also had ceremonial importance, being employed in innumerable rituals of social and civil life. They have fed the imaginations of poets, composers and writers. Transformed into religious terms they provided constant inspiration for the Old Masters. Their colours and scents speak volumes every time we stroll down the garden path in summertime. And in the East each month of the year is symbolized by a particular bloom. The Chinese and Japanese have their own calendars of floral decoration as follows:

Month	*China*	*Japan*
January	Prunus	Pine
February	Peach Blossom	Plum Blossom
March	Tree peony	Peach blossom
April	Cherry blossom	Cherry blossom
May	Magnolia	Wistaria
June	Pomegranate	Iris
July	Lotus	Morning glory

Month	*China*	*Japan*
August	Pear blossom	Lotus
September	Mallow	Seven herbal grasses
October	Chrysanthemum	Maple
November	Gardenia	Chrysanthemum
December	Poppy	Camellia

Old English writers noted how certain plants were closely linked with each of the twelve months, the laurustinus with January and the dainty snowdrop with February; March had its shamrock, next came the daffodil or Lent lily. Throughout the entire year each of the seasons contributed to the satisfaction of the religious and aesthetic senses of mankind.

Christmas sees the inevitable evergreens, holly, rosemary, laurel, bay and ivy. The holly was long regarded by the peoples of northern climes as a sacred emblem "which preserved nature through the desolation of winter." There is in fact no season of the year when one is completely denied the pleasure provided by flowers, foliage and berries, therefore we shall create a floral calendar of our own.

Flower of January: Gorse (Ulex eurapaeus)

"When gorse is out of bloom, kissing is out of season." Gorse is a perennial which flourishes throughout the year, it is therefore a favourite floral emblem for the month of January, a time when the fields and gardens are denuded of flower life. The golden yellow blossom of the gorse carpeting the heathlands wafts its warm exciting perfume on the winds for miles. Sailors far out at sea have been welcomed by its scent as they return to their homeland.

Gorse has a wide variety of uses. It can be made into wine, and the stems are sometimes whittled by countrymen into walking sticks. Among its folk names we find such curiosities as French fuzz, honey bottle and suss. Gorse is a lucky flower for those born on November 28th.

Flower of February: Snowdrop (Galanthus nivalis)

The pretty snowdrop, known sometimes as Eve's tears, February fair maid, dewdrops and dingle dell, is so named because of its resemblance to the snowflake and also to a similarity to the long ear pendants or drops worn by fashionable ladies in the sixteenth and seventeenth centuries.

The snowdrop symbolizes friendship in adversity, and by wearing one of the blossoms you become endowed with pure and lofty thoughts, doubtless because the flowers bloom about the time of the Feast of the Purification. The snowdrop is the birthday flower for those born on January 20th.

Flower of March: Daffodil (Narcissus)

> . . . daffodils
> That come before the swallow dares, and take
> The winds of March with beauty
> Shakespeare, *The Winter's Tale*

The graceful daffodil, the yellow flower which bejewels our gardens in early spring, is the inspiration behind much lyrical verse, yet curiously it was once thought unlucky, due perhaps to its legendary associations with Narcissus and Prosperina, the goddess of sleep and death, and also to its narcotic properties which made it "the flower of deceit". Today, these sad attributes forgotten, we universally join in its worship.

The daffodil is the emblem of chivalry and the birthday flower of those born on August 23rd.

Flower of April: Tulip (Tulipa)

The great majority of tulips were introduced from the Near East, being known in European Turkey as early as the sixteenth century. They were adopted by the English and found a niche in national folklore where they became known as fairies' cradles. The red tulip is the June 7th birthday flower and, needless to say, is one of the symbols of ardent love. Alas, the yellow tulip symbolizes hopeless love. A tulip tree in blossom is the emblem of rural happiness.

Flower of May: The Daisy (Bellis perennis)

> We meet thee like a pleasant thought.
> Wordsworth, "To A Daisy"

In the march of the grand army of flowers across the fields of springtime we find that tiny emblem of rural innocence, the daisy or day's eye. It is not easy to associate the modest daisy with violence, yet its true name is *Bellis*, the Latin for war. The daisy became so named because of its use as a medicinal herb for the staunching of wounds. It is also known as baby's pet and Miss Modesty. The daisy is the birthday flower of those born on April 17th.

Flower of June: The Rose (Rosacae)

> The rose is the fairest flower of all
> That evermore was or evermore shall.
>
> From an old carol

The rose, the traditional emblem of England, is dedicated to love today as it was to Venus in ancient times, hence the symbolism of the bridal rose, happy love.

There are many legends to account for its origins; one of the most beautiful from Rumanian folklore tells us how the god Jupiter transformed a beautiful young girl into the first rose bush.

The rose is the birthday flower for April 26th. The white rose is the July 8th birthday flower and symbolizes spirituality, virginity and silence.

Flower of July: Carnation (Dianthus caryophyllus)

> The fields about the city fair
> Were all with roses set.
> Gillyflowers and carnations fair
> Which canker could not fret.
>
> From an old ballad

The carnation, the birthday flower for those born on December 19th, is also the Christian symbol of pure marriage. According to an ancient legend the world's first carnation burst into bloom on the day Christ was born and the flower has remained from that time forth one of the emblems of love. A festive flower, it has been worn by groomsmen at weddings and has even been served up at banquets, candied and pickled. It has also done service as a spice to flavour the wine.

Flower of August: Foxglove (Digitalis purpurea)

The Foxglove on fair Flora's hand is worn
Lest while she gathers flowers she meet a thorn.
A. Cowley

The foxglove is an admittedly furtive flower, hence no doubt its symbolism in the Language of Flowers: "Insincerity". The tallness of the stalks, the glove-shaped corolla, plus the poisonous leaves, enhance the melodramatic atmosphere surrounding this sinister plant. To our ancestors the sap of the foxglove could be used as a potion to dispose of fairy children, known as changelings, which were left on one's doorstep, so to speak.

Among its folk names we find deadman's bells, bloody bells, flop top, flowster-docken and the inevitable foxfingers. The foxglove is the birthday flower for those born on August 31st.

Flower of September: Dahlia (Dahlia variabilis)

The dahlia you brought to our Isle,
Your praises for ever shall speak
Mid gardens as sweet as your smile
And in colour as bright as your cheek.

In these fulsome terms was Dr Dahl thanked for introducing the dahlia into England, and as members of innumerable dahlia societies assure us, it is an aristocrat among garden flowers, the embodiment of noble attributes.

As the symbol of dignity, elegance and, alas, instability, the dahlia is the birthday flower for those born on August 24th.

Flower of October: Michaelmas Daisy (Aster)

The attic star so named in Grecian use . . . .
Rapin

The garden species seen in Britain is an immigrant from America which has taken root in our hearts. The European species was duly honoured by the poet Virgil with the words: "The altars of the gods were once adorned with these flowers." Strange to say, asters languished unloved and almost unnoticed for centuries, being planted in out of the way corners of old gardens. However, the best known variety acquired fame under the name "Remembrance" when it was dedicated to the dead of World War I.

Known also as star wort, the Michaelmas daisy is curiously not a birthday flower, which is understandable considering that in the Language of Love it means "afterthought".

Tree of November: Mountain Ash or Rowan (Sorbus aucaparia)

Rowan tree and red thread
Haud the witches au' in dread.
Old proverb

In flowerless November pride of place should be given to the mountain ash, a symbol of good luck. Red is the traditional antidote to evil, especially witchcraft, so decorate your mountain ash with red ribbon in lieu of flowers to keep the sinister sisterhood out of the home. The rowan is the symbol of hospitality and one of the Celtic trees of life. A favourite among creatures of the wild, it inspired the pleasing fourteenth-century lines:

Glen of the Rowan trees with scarlet berries
With fruit praised by every flock of birds.
A slumbrous paradise for every badger
In their quiet burrow with their young.

The rowan has many charming local names ranging from chit-chat to wiggy dur.

Flowers of Christmas

Christmas, the joyous period of the year
Now with bright holly all your temples strew
With laurel green and sacred mistletoe.
John Gay

As one would expect, the flowers of Christmastime are closely involved in the legendary sense with the birthday of Jesus Christ. The poinsettia with its lovely scarlet hue is a fitting emblem of this season, and is known in Mexico where it first grew as the Flower of the Holy Night.

Then there is the Christmas rose which French children are

Christmas

told sprang from the earth at the touch of the Angel Gabriel's staff. However, it is the evergreens with their scarlet berries which dominate the festive season – the mistletoe, the holly and the ivy.

Church decoration at this time of the year is extremely beautiful and offers an especially festive welcome to visitors. Here we may see a Star of Bethlehem made from everlasting flowers with its background of red immortelles and circle of box holly or evergreen oak. The star is usually displayed in a conspicuous place either in the chancel or adorning the front of the pulpit. The pillars of the nave are decorated with spiralling wreaths of evergreen.

Finally there are to be seen the cross and anchor, the symbols of atonement and patience, beautiful and memorable, decorated with dark evergreen leaves, and of course holly, the emblem of domestic happiness and the symbol of the Passion of Jesus Christ.

Bibliography

BARRACLOUGH, DAPHNE, *A Flower-Lover's Miscellany*: Frederick Warne Ltd, 1961.

BEALS, KATHERINE M., *Flower Lore and Legend*: Henry Holt & Co., New York, 1917.

BOLTON, BRETT L., *The Secret Power of Plants*: Sphere Books Ltd, 1975.

BOWNESS, CHARLES, *Romany Magic*: The Aquarian Press, 1974.

BRAND, JOHN, *Observations Upon Popular Antiquities*: London, 1849.

BROWNING, GARETH H., *Children's Book of Garden Flowers* (first series): W. & R. Chambers Ltd, 1927.

BROWNING, GARETH H., *Children's Book of Wild Flowers* (second series): W. & R. Chambers Ltd, 1930.

BURNE, C.E., *The Handbook of Folklore*: Sidgwick & Jackson Ltd, 1914.

COATS, ALICE M., *Flowers and Their Histories*: A. & C. Black Ltd, 1956.

CONNELL, CHARLES, *Aphrodisiacs In Your Garden*: Arthur Barker Ltd, 1965.

DUTTON, RALPH, *The English Garden*: B.T. Batsford Ltd, 1937.

ELLIS, AYTOUN, *The Essence of Beauty*: Secker & Warburg Ltd, 1960.

ELLIS, E.S., *Ancient Anodynes*: Heinemann Medical Books Ltd, 1946.

FOLKARD, RICHARD, *Plant Lore, Legends & Lyrics* (second series): Sampson Low, 1892.

GERARD, JOHN, *The Herball or General Historie of Plantes*: London, 1636.

GIFFORD, E.S., *The Charms of Love*: Faber & Faber, 1962.

GRIGSON, GEOFFREY, *The Englishman's Flora*: Phoenix House, 1960.

HADFIELD, MILES & JOHN, *Gardens of Delight*: Cassell, 1964.

HATFIELD, AUDREY WYNNE, *How To Enjoy Your Weeds*: Frederick Muller Ltd, 1969.

HAZLETT, W. CAREW, *Fairies & Folklore*: Reeves & Turner, 1905.

HIBBERD, SHIRLEY, *Wild Flowers Through the Seasons*: Collingridge, 1931.

HOLE, CHRISTINA, *English Folklore*: B.T. Batsford Ltd, 1940.

HUTCHINSON, JOHN AND MELVILLE, RONALD, *The Story of Plants and Their Uses To Man*: Waverley Book Co., 1948.
HYAMS, EDWARD AND SMITH, EDWIN, *English Cottage Gardens*: T. Nelson & Sons Ltd, 1970.
INGLIS, BRIAN, *Fringe Medicine*: Faber & Faber Ltd, 1964.
JACOB, DOROTHY, *A Witch's Guide to Gardening*: Paul Elek Ltd, 1964.
JOBES, GERTRUDE, *Dictionary of Mythology, Folklore & Symbols*: Scarecrow Press, New York, 1962.
KANE, HENRY B., *Plants That Changed the World*: Phoenix House, 1962.
KEBLE-MARTIN, W., *The Concise British Flora*: Michael Joseph Ltd, 1965.
KERR, JESSICA, *Shakespeare's Flowers*: Longman Young Books Ltd.
KIRBY, M. & E., *Talks About Trees*: Cassell, Petter & Galpin.
LEMON, KENNETH, *The Golden Age of Plant Hunters*: Phoenix House, 1968.
LUCKIESH, MATTHEW, *Colour and Colours*: D. Van Nostrand Co. Inc., New York, 1938.
MAPLE, ERIC, *Superstition and the Superstitious*: W. H. Allen, 1961.
MAPLE, ERIC, *The Magic of Perfume*: The Aquarian Press, 1973.
MARVIN, D.E., *Curiosities in Proverbs*: G.P. Putnam's Sons, New York, 1916.
NORRIS, DAVID AND CHARROTT-LODWIDGE, J., *The Book of Spells*: Lorrimer Publishing Co., 1974.
The Oxford Book of Garden Flowers: Oxford University Press, 1968.
PORTEOUS, ALEXANDER, *Forest Folklore*: George Allen & Unwin Ltd, 1928.
ST BARBE BAKER, RICHARD, *I Planted Trees*: Lutterworth Press, 1947.
SKINNER, C.M., *Myths and Legends of Trees, Fruit and Plants*: J.B. Lippincott Company, Philadelphia, 1925.
SLADE, M. AND HAMOND, D., *I Have a House*: Harvill Press Ltd, 1950.
THISTLETON-DYER, T.F., *The Folklore of Plants*: Chatto & Windus Ltd, 1889. Reissued by Singing Tree Press, Michigan, 1968.
THISTLETON-DYER, T.F., *The Folklore of Shakespeare*: Dover Publications Inc., New York, 1966.
WATSON, LYALL, *Supernature*: Hodder & Stoughton Ltd, 1973.

Index

Index